MW00973440

Ultimate 2013 WordPress Themes and Plugins

60+ Reviews and 190+ total Plugins and Themes!

Disclaimer

Every effort has been made to make our books and reports as accurate as possible. However, there may be mistakes, both typographical and in content. This content should be used as a general guide and not as the solution.

The author and publisher shall have neither liability nor responsibility to any person or entity with respect to any loss or damage alleged to be caused directly or indirectly by information provided in this report or book.

This report is Copyright ©2013 by Lambert Klein

All Rights Reserved

Introduction

Welcome to the *Ultimate 2013 WordPress Themes and Plugins Guide*! This guide goes over the hottest themes and plugins for 2013. Whether you have a business website, blog, or online store, this guide will come in handy. Choosing the right plugins is incredibly important for your website to reach its full potential. We'll take a look at their pros and cons and show you which ones will enhance your WordPress website, making it easier to use, better looking, and more profitable.

This is an unbiased guide. None of the chosen plugins and themes were selected due to any favoritism on my part, and I'm not being compensated by any software creators to promote them. Each selected plugin and theme was thoroughly researched and deemed to be either one of the best in its particular category or noteworthy for some other reason. I will also go over any negative attributes a plugin or theme might have and recommend alternatives that you may also want to try.

All prices listed in this guide are subject to change. This goes for the star ratings as well. (These aren't my personal rankings; they're taken from the sources where the plugin or theme is available online. All ratings included are on a scale of one to five stars.) This is to give greater insight into the quality of these themes and plugins, since the ratings come from the many people who've downloaded and used the plugins extensively. I do also offer my own opinions, of course.

It should be mentioned that this guide assumes that you already know how to set up WordPress and understand the general idea of what plugins and themes are. If you're completely new to this, go check out my other book, *WordPress Domination*, by typing the following URL into your browser.

`http://www.amazon.com/dp/B007LS0TLE`

It will teach you everything you need to know about web development using WordPress. It is *very* beginner-friendly, but also has neat tips and tricks appropriate for more advanced users as well.

Also, be aware that this guide is intended for use with the WordPress.org website builder. WordPress.com, the free blogging platform, works a bit differently, and the options for it are much more limited.

I'm sure you'll find this guide helpful in getting your site ready for a big year in 2013. Some of the plugins you have come to rely upon might be outdated, or there may be new plugins and themes that do a better job. *The Ultimate 2013 WordPress Themes and Plugins Guide* will uncover all the facts and help make sure you're on the right track to making your website the best it can be.

Note: The themes and plugins listed in the book may have long URLs to enter. If some of them are too long then there are two other options that you can use.

1. Just search for them on the following sites:

Themes
- ThemeGrade.com
  ThemeForest.net
- NewWPThemes.com
- ElegantThemes.com
- WooThemes.com
- SMThemes.com
- ThemeFuse.com
- TemplateMonster.com
- ThemifyMe.com/themes

Plugins
- CodeCanyon.net
- WordPress.org/extend/plugins
- Yoast.com/WordPress
- StudioPress.com/plugins
- ElegantThemes.com/plugins

2. **Download the PDF version of this book**. This way you can click on the links and will be taken directly to the product of your choice. **This is probably the easiest option**. You can download the PDF below.

   Just enter the URL below into your browser.

`http://www.lambertklein.com/wppt.pdf`

Before we get started with the meat of the guide, though, let's go over how to install themes and plugins, just to make sure we're all on the same page!

How to Install WordPress Themes, Step By Step

Installing WordPress themes is fairly straightforward. However, there are several ways to do it. We're going to go over the two most common methods, which should be sufficient to install practically any WordPress theme.

Upload Using the Search Function

By far the easiest way to install a WordPress theme is to do it from the WordPress admin dashboard. When doing this, you can either use the search function, or upload directly from your hard drive if you acquired the theme from other sources.

Here's a step-by-step tutorial of how to use the search feature to install WordPress themes:

Step 1: Getting to the Theme Finder

Go into your WordPress dashboard and look to the left side of the screen. You will see a tab that says "Appearance." Click this and it will create a drop-down box beneath it with more options. Click "Themes." On the new page, look up top and click the tab that says "Install Themes."

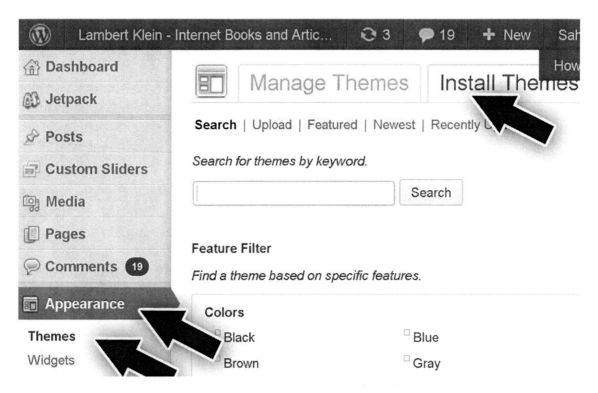

Step 2: Searching for a Theme

You can now search for a theme by using the search box. Also, looking down below, you'll see several options that allow you to refine your search by color, subject, dimensions, and more.

Once you have an idea of what you want, type your keyword in the search box. For example, if you want a magazine-style theme, type in "magazine," then click the "Search" button.

Search for themes by keyword.

	Search

Feature Filter

Find a theme based on specific features.

Colors

☐ Black   ☐ Blue

☐ Brown   ☐ Gray

On the new page, you will see a variety of themes that match your search criteria. All of them should be free and can be installed by simply clicking the "Install Now" button beneath them. You can also preview them by clicking the "Preview" button.

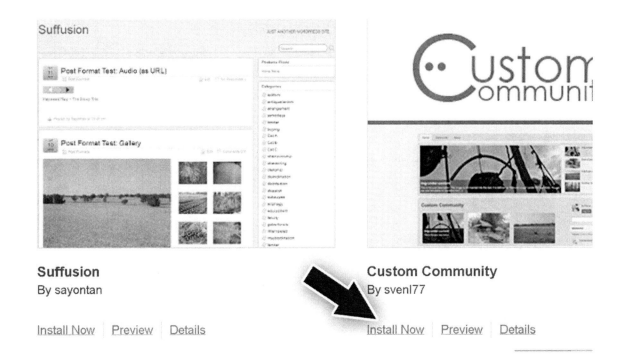

Suffusion
By sayontan

Install Now | Preview | Details

Custom Community
By svenl77

Install Now | Preview | Details

Step 3: Other Options

Before installing a theme, note that there are many other options in the theme finder. For example, you can change your search box from being keyword-based to searching for authors or specific tags associated with themes by using the drop-down box next to the search box.

Also, you will notice several more options at the top: Upload, Featured, Newest, and Recently Updated. These are pretty self-explanatory, but we'll go over how the Upload feature works below.

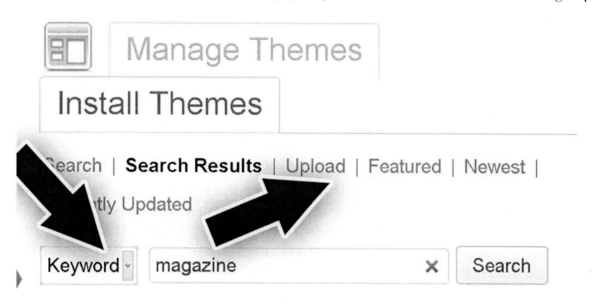

Uploading from Your Hard Drive

The Upload option allows you to upload a theme directly from your hard drive. This is great for when you have purchased or downloaded a theme from the Internet to your computer. The process is straightforward; you browse your computer for the file you want, and then click "Install Now."

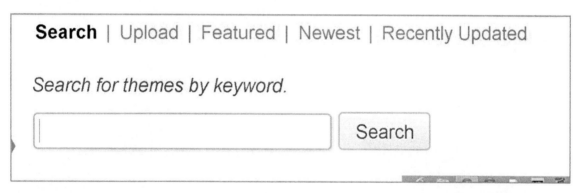

Uploading a Theme Using File Transfer Protocol (FTP)

Now that WordPress allows you to upload themes from your hard drive using the dashboard, this method is somewhat out of date. However, if you want to do it this way, or if the built-in WordPress upload function isn't working for some reason, using FTP is always an option. Be aware that you will need a program like Filezilla to do this. You can download it for free by entering the following URL into your browser.

`http://filezilla-project.org/`

Step 1: Connecting to the Server

The first thing you need to do is open your FTP program and connect to your hosting server. Depending on what program you're using and who your hosting provider is, the way you do this may vary, but most of the time, you'll type in your hosting server's IP address, your username, and your password. Keep in mind that the username and password will be the ones associated with your hosting server's control panel, not your WordPress username and password.

Step 2: Getting into Your WordPress Files

Once connected to the server, you'll then select your domain and get into its files. In most cases, you will follow this directory path: Root Directory » Public HTML » Your Domain » WP-Content » Themes.

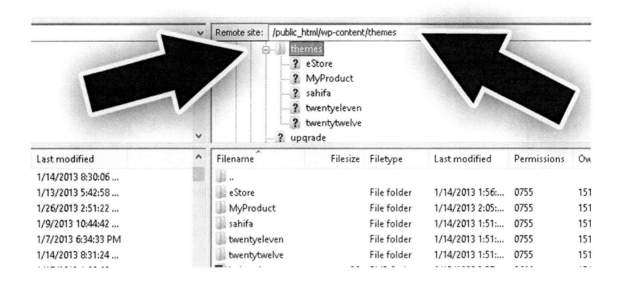

Step 3: Transferring the Files

You'll then select the theme files from your computer and transfer them to your theme folder using the FTP program. You don't have to transfer the files individually; you can usually just send the whole folder over. Just make sure that, if the folder is zipped, to unzip it first.

In most cases, transferring is as simple as right-clicking on the folder you want and then clicking "Upload." If you screw up and transfer something you don't want, select the file in the themes folder, right-click, and delete it. Just be aware that anything you delete from your website is gone for good unless it has been backed up on your hard drive or on your server somewhere.

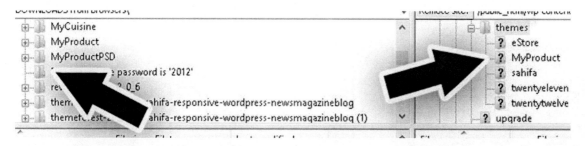

Once you're done with the transfer, close the connection. An FTP connected to your server's database can be a security risk if left open.

How to Activate and Manage Your Themes

Getting your theme uploaded is just the first step; now you have to activate it. Fortunately, this is easy. Go to your WordPress dashboard, click Appearance » Themes, and then the "Manage Themes" tab if it isn't already selected. You should see your new theme on this page. You can install it by clicking "Activate," or preview it first if you want by clicking "Live Preview."

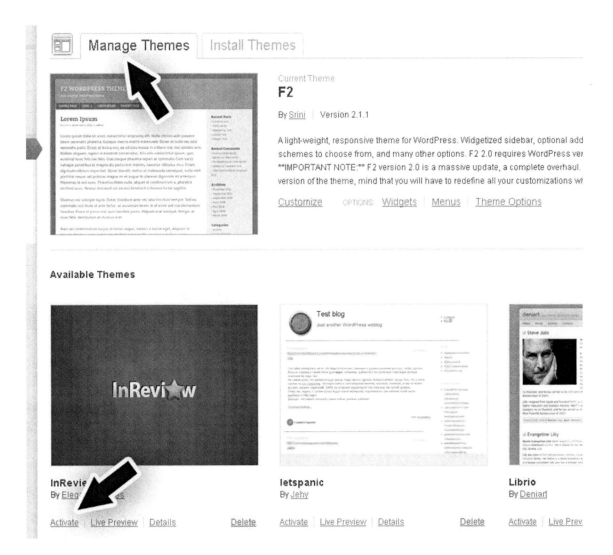

Once your preferred theme is live, it should be displayed at the top of the Manage Themes page. Depending on your theme, you may find some configuration options here. Themes can be configured in a wide variety of ways; some even send you to different locations in the dashboard to access their options. If you can't figure out how to configure your theme, be sure to read the instructions. If they aren't on the Manage Themes page in WordPress, they can usually be found on the creator's website.

Also, be aware that themes sometimes need updates. This could be due to the creator coming up with a superior version, eliminating bugs, or because the theme is no longer compatible with the current version of WordPress. If your theme needs an update, a notification will often appear in your dashboard. If your theme abruptly stops working, check for an update on the creator's site. If the creator has stopped updating the theme, it may end up becoming obsolete.

Warning about CSS and PHP

Just about all themes allow you to edit their CSS and PHP files, letting you customize them further. Some even encourage it. However, unless you understand how to edit these file types, I don't recommend that you do so. Screwing up the CSS and PHP can lead to your theme not functioning anymore.

If you are going to edit these files, make sure you back your theme up first. If you downloaded your theme to your hard drive, then you already have a backup. However, if you downloaded it using the WordPress dashboard, you need to copy your theme files onto your hard drive. You can do this with a FTP program, as we discussed earlier, only you'd be transferring files from your server's database to your hard drive.

If you ever break the CSS or PHP, you can always re-upload your theme if you have it backed up. However, you'll lose any changes or customizations you've made if you do.

Donating

A lot of themes are free and the creators don't charge anything for their use. However, many creators do have "donate" buttons on their websites that you can use to show your appreciation for their hard work. If you find a free theme you really enjoy, consider making a donation to the creator as a way of saying thanks.

How to Install Plugins, Step By Step

Installing plugins for WordPress works almost identically to installing themes: you can either do it through the dashboard or you can use an FTP program to get the job done.

Uploading Plugins Using the Plugin Finder

You can upload plugins from the dashboard either through using the search function or directly from your hard drive, just like with themes.

Step 1: Getting to the Plugin Finder

Click on the tab on the left-hand menu that says "Plugins," then click the option on the new drop-down menu that says "Add New." A new page will open up, giving you a search bar and some extra options up top that we'll go over in a moment.

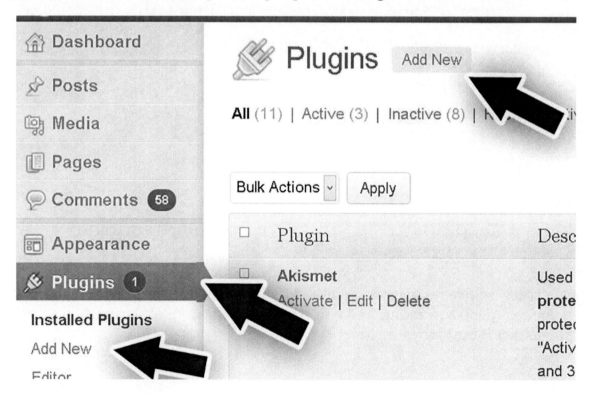

Step 2: Searching for a Plugin

Start by typing the keyword that you want, and then click the "Search Plugins" button. For example, if you wanted an anti-spam plugin, type in "anti-spam" and click the button.

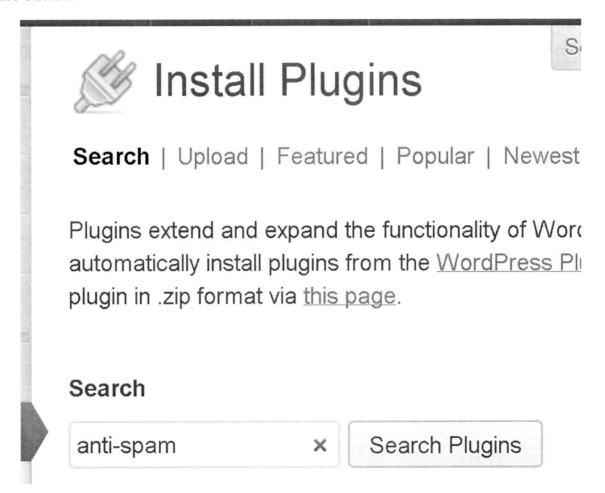

A new screen will come up with several plugins to choose from. Each listed plugin has a version number, a rating, and a description. Take note of these when selecting the plugin that is best for your site.

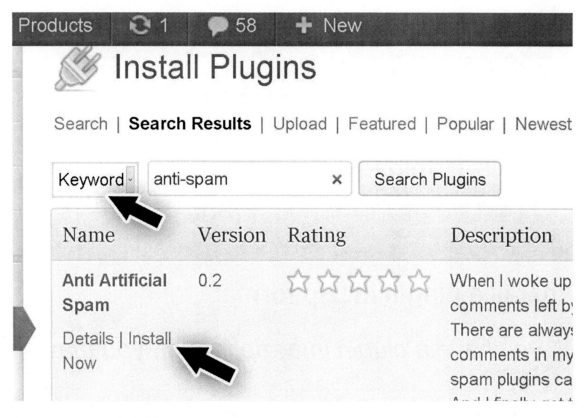

Step 3: Other Options

Once again, you'll see some other options above the search bar: Upload, Featured, Popular, Newest, and Favorites. As with themes, the Upload option can be used to upload plugins directly from your hard drive.

Install Plugins

Search | **Upload** | Featured | Popular | Ne

Install a plugin in .zip format

If you have a plugin in a .zip format, you may

Choose File   No file chosen

Uploading from your Hard Drive

Just like with themes, you'll click the "Upload" option and select the plugin you want from your hard drive, and then click "Install Now."

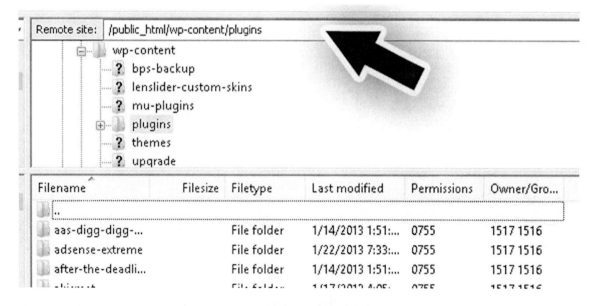

Uploading a Plugin Using File Transfer Protocol

Aside from putting plugins into your Plugins folder, this is no different from uploading themes. Again, you'll need a program like Filezilla to do this.

Step 1: Connecting to the Server

Connect to your hosting server, usually by entering an IP address, username, and password. The username and password should be the ones associated with your control panel, though it might vary for different hosting services.

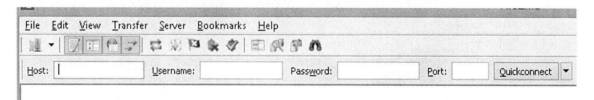

Step 2: Getting into Your WordPress Files

This is very straightforward. The file path is Root » Public HTML » Your Domain Name » WP-Content » Plugins.

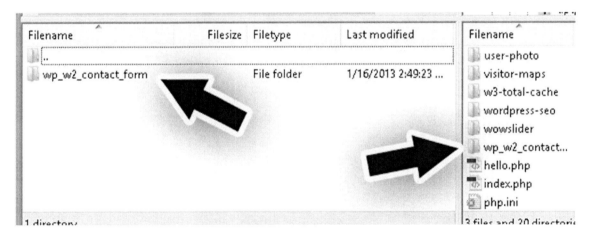

Step 3: Transferring the Files

Find the plugin files on your hard drive, right-click the folder, and select "Upload." Make sure you have the plugins folder selected in your server database first, or it will go into the wrong folder. Also, be aware that you can transfer the entire folder at once, but zipped files will need to be unzipped first.

Once this is complete, close your FTP program; leaving it open can become a security risk.

Activating and Managing Your Plugins

Unlike themes, some plugins activate automatically as soon as you install them from the dashboard. However, others will need to be activated manually.

To activate a plugin, click the "Plugins" tab on the left side of the dashboard. You will be taken to a list of all of your installed plugins. Beneath the name of each plugin you'll see various options, including "Activate" for plugins that are not yet active. Clicking "Activate" will activate an inactive plugin.

Just activating a plugin isn't always enough to get it working. Some plugins also need to be configured. This can get somewhat tricky, due to the fact that the configuration options for a plugin can appear in various locations in the dashboard. Sometimes they appear in the plugin list; sometimes they appear somewhere in the left-hand menu. If you can't find a plugin's configuration options, check the creator's website for instructions.

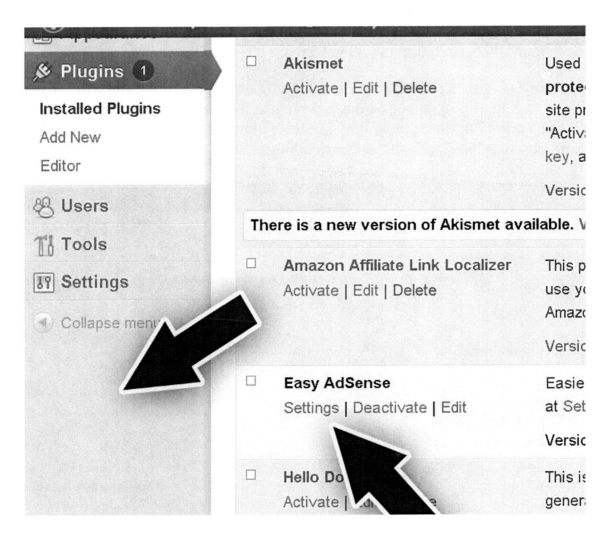

Keep in mind that you can deactivate and delete plugins from the plugin page at any time. This is good for getting rid of obsolete plugins that are no longer supported by their creator or for disabling plugins that may be conflicting with your theme or other plugins.

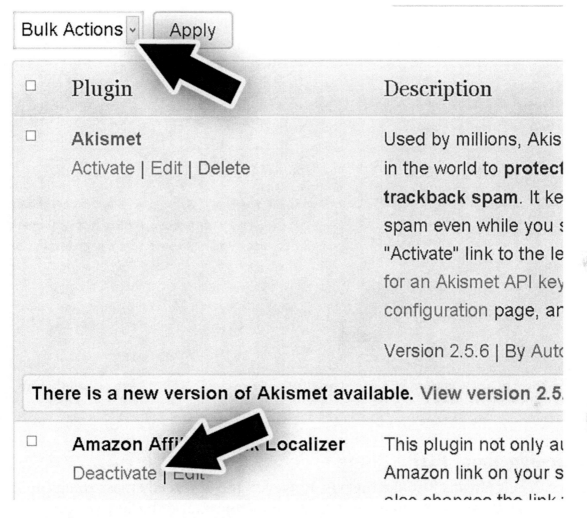

Plugins tend to need updates more frequently than themes. When one or more plugins need to be updated, a number will appear next to the Plugins tab in the left-hand menu indicating how many plugins need updates. When you go to the plugins page, you can more easily view which plugins need to be updated by clicking the option up at the top that says "Update Available." To update a plugin, click on the option next to it that says, "Update now."

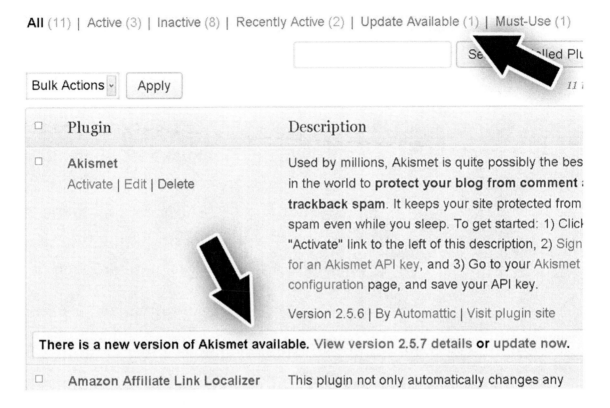

Warning about PHP Editing

You can edit plugins just like themes. However, this can really mess things up if you don't know what you're doing. It is especially important to backup plugins that you paid for before doing this. Also, be aware that screwing this up can have wildly unpredictable effects on your website. Only do this if you know exactly what you're doing.

Donating

Just as with themes, a lot of plugins are available for free online. The creators of these plugins have worked hard to bring you quality ways to enhance your WordPress site. Some plugins will have a little "donate" option, either on the Plugin page in the dashboard or on the creator's website itself. If you enjoy a plugin and have money to spare, I encourage you to donate what you can to the creator as a way of showing your appreciation for his or her hard work.

All-Purpose Plugins

The following plugins work well with just about any type of WordPress website. Whether you're building an online store or just want to make a really cool blog, these plugins will help you make your site the best it can be by enhancing various general features. A few of these were spotlighted in my other books, _WordPress Domination_ and _WordPress Security_ listed below, but we go over a ton more here.

```
http://www.amazon.com/WordPress-Domination-Beginner-
Wordpress-ebook/dp/B007LS0TLE
```

```
http://www.amazon.com/WordPress-Security-Protection-
Crackers-ebook/dp/B007TTSU0W/
```

To visit the download page for each plugin, simply type their URL into your browser. Enjoy!

> **Download the PDF version of this book**. This way you can click on the links and will be taken directly to the product of your choice. **This is probably the easiest option**. You can download the PDF below.
>
> Just enter the URL below into your browser.

```
http://www.lambertklein.com/wppt.pdf
```

W3 Total Cache

Price

Free

Description

W3 Total Cache is a plugin designed to help WordPress sites load faster. It uses a memory-based cache known as memcache. It also does other things, such as offering options for content delivery networks and compressing the file size of your web pages, making them easier to download.

W3 Total Cache

`http://wordpress.org/extend/plugins/w3-total-cache/`

Pros

- One of the fastest caching plugins available
- Compresses your web pages' file sizes for easy download
- Caching options for content delivery networks can help when your web content is posted to social media sites

Cons

- Not all servers are immediately compatible with memcache, which means you may have to go through some additional steps to get it set up
- Advanced options take good knowledge of CSS to use
- Adds a long footnote to your source code that takes some work to remove

Rating

W3 Total Cache is extremely popular and has received a rating of 4.6 out of 5 stars. It has over 2,400 five-star votes.

Conclusion

W3 Total Cache will make your website load super-fast, but it does take some technical know-how to get the most out of it. If you're great with CSS, this could be an amazing plugin for you. If not, you may want something simpler to work with.

Alternate Options

<u>WP-Super Cache</u>

`http://wordpress.org/extend/plugins/wp-super-cache/`

— This is a very popular caching plugin that's been around for a while. Not as fast as W3 Total Cache, but still very reliable and easy to use.

Widget Logic

Price

Free

Description

By default, WordPress will normally have your widgets and sidebar options appear on every page. This plugin lets you determine which pages your widgets appear on, giving you greater control over the overall layout of your website.

Widget Logic

```
http://wordpress.org/extend/plugins/widget-logic/
```

Pros

- Very easy-to-use control field for selecting the pages you want your widgets on
- Has an option for tweaking a widget's HTML

Cons

- The plugin operates through the use of something known as EVAL. Anyone who has the ability to edit widgets on your site can introduce malicious code if they choose.

Rating

Widget Logic currently has a high rating of 4.2 out of 5 stars. It has received over 360 five-star ratings.

Conclusion

Widget Logic lives up to its intent and does a very good job. If you want more control over your widgets, this is a great plugin. The security flaw is a minor issue so long as you're the only one allowed to access your WordPress dashboard.

Alternate Options

<u>Widget Context</u>

`http://wordpress.org/extend/plugins/widget-context/`

- While not as popular as Widget Logic, this plugin is actually rated slightly higher, at 4.6 out of 5 stars. Compatibility issues may be an issue with WordPress 3.5 and later.

<u>Sidebar and Widget Manager for WordPress</u>

`http://codecanyon.net/item/sidebar-widget-manager-for-wordpress/2287447`

- This plugin is a bit more advanced than the free ones and has a variety of options, such as the ability to create custom layouts, the ability to drop widgets into page content, variable alignment options, and unlimited custom sidebars. It also requires no coding. It costs $15 for the regular license (for personal websites) and $75 for the extended license (for template creation).

Hint: Go to codecanyon.net and search for this plugin if you rather not type this long URL into your browser. You can do this with other long URLs as well.

WordPress Ajax Contact Form

Price

Regular License - $12

Extended license not currently available.

Description

WordPress Ajax Contact Form is a contact form creation plugin, as its name suggests. Unlike most free variants, this plugin comes with lots of options, including multiple- or single-recipient systems, multiple or single attachments, a script based on open-source framework, a drag-and-drop anti-spam system, reCaptcha integration, and AYAH integration.

WordPress Ajax Contact Form

`http://codecanyon.net/item/wordpress-ajax-contact-form-with-attachments/3463740`

Pros

- Very easy to use
- Easy to customize, since it is based on open-source framework
- Drag-and-drop anti-spam system is very user-friendly
- Extremely flexible overall
- Tons of options and features

Cons

- The many options may seem overwhelming to newbies.

Rating

WordPress Ajax Contact Form currently has a buyer rating of 4 out of 5 stars.

Conclusion

Overall, this is a handy all-in-one contact form creation system. It has practically everything you could ever want wrapped up in one plugin. The only drawback is that if you're new to WordPress or configuring plugins, all those options may seem a bit overwhelming. Still, for only $12 this is an excellent plugin, though the lack of an extended license may be disappointing if you're a web developer.

Alternate Options

Contact Form 7

```
http://wordpress.org/extend/plugins/contact-form-7/
```

– Considered one of the top dogs when it comes to contact form creation, Contact Form 7 is very flexible and easy to use. It is currently rated at 4.3 out of 5 stars. The only drawback is that its options are somewhat limited, forcing you to use other plugins such as Flamingo, Really Simple CAPTCHA, and Bogo to get the most out of it. It's still an extremely good contact form creator considering that it's free.

QuForm

```
http://codecanyon.net/item/quform-wordpress-form-
builder/706149
```

– This plugin has gotten a lot of attention lately and currently has a five-star buyer rating. It resembles WordPress Ajax Contact Form in many ways but features an easy-to-use drag-and-drop creation system. It is a bit more expensive at $25 for a regular license (no extended license available, unfortunately), but seems to offer a bit more flexibility than Ajax.

Gravity Forms

```
http://www.gravityforms.com/
```

– This up-and-coming plugin prides itself on being one of the fastest and easiest to use form plugins available. It also boasts the ability to integrate with several popular web resources, such as PayPal, Aweber, MailChimp, CampaignMonitor, and more. It also has features like a visual form editor, multi-page forms, condition fields and order form capability. On top of all this, Gravity Forms has been pre-optimized to work with several popular theme providers, like Headway Themes, Woo Themes, and Allure Themes.

While slightly lacking the overall capability of QuForm and Ajax, Gravity Forms is still massively popular and currently installed on over half a million WordPress sites.

This is probably due to its compatibility with PayPal and the other themes and properties listed above. It costs $39 for the standard license, which may be worth it if you want something already pre-optimized for a certain theme or to work with Aweber or MailChimp

HTML5 Video Player

Price

Regular License - $20

Extended License not currently available

Description

HTML5 Video Player makes it easy to display videos on your WordPress site without having to rely upon external sources like YouTube. It also allows the creation of a right-side video playlist, or a bottom playlist if you choose. It is the only HTML5 video player currently compatible with Android.

(I want to emphasize that, despite my name, I have no connection to the Lambert Group that created this plugin.)

HTML5 Video Player

```
http://codecanyon.net/item/html5-video-player-wordpress-
plugin/1613464
```

Pros

- Multiple skins to choose from
- Can have a right-side or bottom video play list
- Compatible with both Android and iOS
- Website has a video tutorial to help you get started
- Plays MP4, Ogg video (OGV), and WebM video files
- Multiple adjustable parameters, such as height and width

Cons

- Doesn't support YouTube videos, only HTTP streaming

Rating

HTML5 Video Player currently has a buyer rating of 4 out of 5 stars.

Conclusion

HTML5 Video Player is one of the big boys when it comes to video plugins. Being fully optimized for mobile sets it apart from older models and really gives it an edge. The $20 price is great for what you get, though the lack of an extended license is disappointing.

Alternate Options

<u>Video Player</u>

```
http://codecanyon.net/item/video-player-wordpress-plugin-
youtubeflvh264/719162
```

– This simply named plugin also comes from the Lambert Group. It's a bit scaled down compared to the HTML5 version, but offers a greater range of compatibility, including YouTube, MP4, M4V, M4A, MOV, MP4v, MP3, and F4V, as well as RTMP compatibility. If you want a player that's more versatile in what type of files it can play, this may be the plugin for you. It is currently rated at 4 out of 5 stars and costs $21.

<u>VidEmbed</u>

```
http://ithemes.com/purchase/vidembed/
```

– This video player plugin allows you to embed video in a variety of places, even in widgets. Other neat features are the shortcode button for quick and easy embedding, various customizable settings, and a one-year subscription that offers premium support and product updates. It works with multiple file types, including FLV, MP4, and MOV formats, in addition to those hosted on Amazon S3 and YouTube. Even better is the fact that a developer license costs only $20, allowing you to use this plugin on sites built for clients as many times as you wish.

<u>Video Gallery</u>

```
http://codecanyon.net/item/video-gallery-wordpress-plugin-w-
youtube-vimeo-/157782
```

– If you want to put entire video galleries on your WordPress site, this is the plugin for you. Its options may be a bit more limited than other video plugins, but it makes up for it by allowing you to create video galleries that are fully optimized for iOS devices. On top of this, it also has an import/export feature, allowing you to backup your database and keep it safe. The regular license is only $15, and the extended license is $75 — something web developers will love.

All in One Favicon

Price

Free

Description

As you probably know, a favicon is that little symbol that appears on tabs you open in your Internet browser. Having a good favicon is a cool way to make your site stand out to visitors. All in One Favicon allows you to add a favicon of your choice quickly and easily. It supports three file types (ICO, PNG, and GIF) and has been localized for a variety of languages, including Spanish, Dutch, French, German, among others.

All in One Favicon

`http://wordpress.org/extend/plugins/all-in-one-favicon/`

Pros

- Add a favicon to your WordPress site quickly and easily.

Cons

- Has not been updated for WordPress 3.5, although it still functions

Rating

This plugin is rated at 4.7 out of 5 stars.

Conclusion

Nothing fancy here. All in One Favicon does what it claims to do: it adds a favicon to your WordPress site. Though it hasn't been updated for WordPress 3.5, it still works. Also, if you're from a non-English speaking country, you'll appreciate the fact that it has been localized for other languages.

Alternate Options

Personal Favicon

```
http://wordpress.org/extend/plugins/personal-favicon/
```

– This plugin doesn't differ much from All in One Favicon, and its rating is slightly lower at 4.6 out of 5. It is very basic and easy to use, getting the job done with no fuss.

Calendarize It

Price

Regular License – $25

Extended License – $125

Description

Calendarize It is a calendar program designed to be very flexible and work with a variety of different types of WordPress websites. It has plenty of options, such as support for custom fields for events, support for reoccurring events, an easy point-and-click interface, and support for shortcodes. Perhaps the best element is the fact that you can take advantage of the "try before you buy" feature by visiting their web page.

Calendarize It

```
http://codecanyon.net/item/calendarize-it-for-
wordpress/2568439
```

Pros

- Designed with a very broad target audience in mind
- Very versatile
- A point-and-click system that's easy to use
- Multiple event scheduling options
- Sidebar mini widget calendar option is very convenient

Cons

- Not designed for the needs of any specific industry
- Huge number of options can be overwhelming

Rating

Calendarize It currently has a buyer rating of 4 out of 5 stars.

Conclusion

Calendarize It is one of the most versatile WordPress calendars available. If you need to keep track of events and dates on your WordPress site, you can't really go wrong with this plugin and its massive amount of options. The only noteworthy drawback is that if you need a calendar for a specific industry, there may be something more specialized for you out there.

Alternate Options

WordPress Pro Event Calendar

`http://codecanyon.net/item/wordpress-pro-event-calendar/2485867`

– This sleek and easy-to-use calendar has several notable features: Google Maps support, cross browser support, and a responsive draggable/touchable interface. The regular license is a great deal at $15, while the extended license is $75.

WordPress Events Calendar

`http://codecanyon.net/item/wordpress-events-calendar/910386`

– This calendar's a bit more scaled down than the others, but is a steal at only $10 for the regular license and $50 for the extended. If you just need a good, basic calendar, this is a great choice.

Calendar

`http://wordpress.org/extend/plugins/calendar/`

– This free calendar is extremely popular and has had nearly 350,000 downloads. It features a variety of handy options, such as mouse-over functionality, various sidebar/widget options, and full internationalization for a broad appeal worldwide.

FontPress

Price

Regular License – $15

Extended License - $75

Description

One of the main limitations of the WordPress website building format is that it doesn't allow you to change fonts. This plugin takes care of that problem and provides you with the ability to add and use unlimited fonts of your choice. It comes with more than thirty fonts already installed and allows you to edit the color, size, and line height of your text.

FontPress

```
http://codecanyon.net/item/fontpress-font-manager-
plugin/1746759
```

Pros

- 30+ fonts to use from the start
- Can upload unlimited custom fonts
- Can edit font attributes, such as color, shadow, size, and more
- Typography shortcode makes it easy to use; no CSS required
- Website offers video tutorials

Cons

- Nothing notable

Rating

FontPress currently has a buyer rating of 5 out of 5 stars.

Conclusion

There really isn't anything not to love about FontPress. It solves all the font issues of WordPress quickly and easily. It even has tutorials on how to use it, making it extremely newbie friendly.

Alternate Options

Use Any Font

`http://wordpress.org/extend/plugins/use-any-font/`

- This free font plugin has several attractive features. It supports compatibility with all the major browsers and operating systems, including mobile ones like Android and iOS. It also has an easy-to-use setup with no CSS needed. Since it stores the fonts on your server, it doesn't impact load times for visitors. There aren't a lot of good free font plugins out there, but this one is a gem.

After the Deadline

Price

Free

Description

WordPress's default spellchecker isn't the greatest. To pick up the slack, After the Deadline is a great choice. It features a contextual spell checker, advanced style checking, and intelligent grammar checking. In addition to all this, it is available on multiple platforms, allowing you to install it in Chrome, Firefox, and more in addition to WordPress. Best of all: it's free!

After the Deadline

`http://www.afterthedeadline.com/`

Pros

- Accurate spelling and grammar checker that utilizes artificial intelligence
- Contextual spelling check is a must for professional writers
- Available on several platforms
- Tutorials on the website make it very newbie-friendly
- Really good value for a free plugin

Cons

- Developer licensing may be a bit restrictive.

Rating

This plugin is rated at 4.6 out of 5 stars.

Conclusion

This free plugin may not have tons of options or features but it really doesn't need them. It's good at what it does and makes writing directly in the WordPress dashboard much easier. The website tutorials will get you up and running with this incredible plugin fast.

Alternate Options

<u>Pro Writing Aid</u>

`http://wordpress.org/extend/plugins/prowritingaid/`

– This free plugin not only looks for spelling and grammar errors, it also checks for overused words, clichés, and redundancies. It is rated 5 out of 5 stars, but only has one rating at this time and hasn't been optimized for WordPress 3.5 yet.

Google XML Sitemaps

Price

Free

Description

Probably the most popular XML sitemap generator at over 9 million downloads, this old favorite gets the job done quickly and easily. It generates a sitemap that helps the crawlers from Google, Bing, Yahoo!, and others to index your website and pages more easily, which is essential when it comes to getting highly ranked in search engines.

Google XML Sitemaps

```
http://wordpress.org/extend/plugins/google-sitemap-
generator/
```

Pros

- Easy to install and use
- Still considered the best XML sitemap plugin by many
- Works without hassle

Cons

- Nothing significant

Rating

4.6 out of 5 stars, with nearly 3,000 five-star ratings.

Conclusion

After all these years, Google XML Sitemaps is still king of the hill. You really can't go wrong with this one.

Alternate Options

XML Sitemap

```
http://wordpress.org/extend/plugins/xml-sitemap-xml-
sitemapcouk/
```

– This free plugin also provides an XML sitemap for the search engines. It is rated 5 out of 5 stars, but only has one rating at this time. It also provides a shortcode for use on HTML sites if you want. It has not yet been optimized for WordPress 3.5 as of this writing.

P3 (Plugin Performance Profiler)

Price

Free

Description

This is a lesser-known plugin that's nevertheless very useful, especially if you're installing lots of plugins on your WordPress site. P3 checks your plugins and looks for performance issues. If a plugin is slowing down your website, P3 will find it and let you know.

P3 Plugin Performance Profiler

`http://wordpress.org/extend/plugins/p3-profiler/`

Pros

- Helps to optimize your website's load time
- Easy to use

Cons

- Only works with certain browsers (Chrome, Firefox, Safari, Opera, IE9)

Rating

This plugin has a rating of 4.6 out of 5 stars.

Conclusion

This is a very handy plugin to have, especially when you're installing a lot of plugins and don't know if they are slowing down your website or not. Those who don't use mainstream browsers might view the limited variety of support available as a drawback.

Alternate Options Nothing notable

Plugins for Search Engine Optimization (SEO)

Search engine optimization is all about satisfying the search engines, particularly Google, so that you can get your website and its pages ranked highly. A higher ranking means more exposure. To help with this, there are plenty of plugins that enhance the various SEO-related factors of your WordPress site.

WP-PageNavi

Price

Free

Description

Internal linking structure and navigation are a big part of SEO these days, so it pays to make sure you can get things set up the way you want. WP-PageNavi makes it easy to structure your internal navigation and linking. It comes with several options, though many people simply install it and let it do its thing.

WP-PageNavi

`http://wordpress.org/extend/plugins/wp-pagenavi/`

Pros

- Very easy to use
- Multiple options to give you complete control over your navigation structure
- Great for SEO

Cons

- Your web host needs to have PHP5 for this to work

Rating

WP-PageNavi has a four-star rating and has been downloaded over 3 million times. It's very popular.

Conclusion

Still considered one of the best navigation plugins around, WP-PageNavi is loved for its simple yet effective design.

Alternate Options

Zamango Page Navigation

`http://wordpress.org/extend/plugins/zamango-page-navigation/`

– This free plugin features a variety of advanced page navigation options and customizability using CSS and HTML. Has a rating of 4.4 out of 5 stars.

GD Pages Navigator

`http://wordpress.org/extend/plugins/gd-pages-navigator/`

– This plugin allows you to edit the hierarchy of the page display as well as a dynamic list of pages, depending on which page is currently displayed. It is also notable that it is configured for both Serbian and English. This plugin is free.

Simple Selection Navigation Widget

`http://wordpress.org/extend/plugins/simple-section-navigation/`

– Another free plugin, this one is rated 4.9 out of 5 stars. Simple Selection Navigation Widget focuses on implementing navigation via widgets, as its name implies. If this is how you want to do navigation, this is a good choice; it has plenty of options to work with.

Breadcrumb NavXT

`http://wordpress.org/extend/plugins/breadcrumb-navxt/`

– This popular free plugin is designed to allow easy page navigation by adding "breadcrumb" trails to posts and pages, linking visitors back to parent categories or pages. These links are great for SEO as well. The plugin comes with over 10 languages installed and is very popular among bloggers and Internet marketers.

Google Analytics for WordPress

Price

Free

Description

Keeping track of your WordPress site's stats is very important, and Google Analytics is one of the best tools out there. This plugin allows you to track tons of metadata about your site, like outbound links and download tracking. It also uses an asynchronous Google Analytics tracking code for exceptionally accurate results.

Google Analytics for WordPress

```
http://wordpress.org/extend/plugins/google-analytics-for-
wordpress/
```

Pros

- Very easy to use
- Tons of options
- Allows you to connect your Google AdSense and Google Analytics accounts
- Installation instructions are available on the website
- Allows tracking of custom variables

Cons

- Nothing notable

Rating

This plugin has a rating of 4.3 out of 5, with close to 4 million downloads.

Conclusion

Google Analytics for WordPress is still considered by many to be the standard for using Google Analytics on WordPress. It can track just about any stat you need, making it easy to see where your site is succeeding and where it needs work. This is a critical part of SEO.

Alternate Options

<u>Google Analytics Dashboard</u>

`http://wordpress.org/extend/plugins/google-analytics-dashboard/`

– This free plugin allows you to display Google Analytics data in your dashboard. It also lets you embed the data onto your site if you want. The major drawback is that you'll need to get a Google Analytics code and then use another plugin, such as Google Analytics for WordPress, to make it work.

<u>Google Analyticator</u>

`http://wordpress.org/extend/plugins/google-analyticator/`

– This one allows you to display your Google Analytics results right there in your dashboard. However, there have been reports of bugs and compatibility issues. Despite this, this free plugin is quite popular and has been downloaded over 2 million times.

WordPress SEO by Yoast

Price

Free

Description

There are a variety of plugins designed to ensure that all SEO criteria on your website are met. This particular plugin is designed by WordPress SEO consultant/designer Joost de Valk (whose first name is pronounced "Yoast"). WordPress SEO by Yoast really goes the extra mile in providing you with a huge arrangement of options, including search engine result previews, in-depth page analysis, automatic WordPress optimization, XML sitemaps, metadata insertion, social integration, breadcrumb integration, and much more. This plugin just about does it all.

WordPress SEO by Yoast

`http://wordpress.org/extend/plugins/wordpress-seo/`

Pros

- Handles just about every SEO factor you could think of
- Massive amount of options and settings
- Designed by a WordPress SEO consultant
- Very easy to use
- Newbie-friendly despite its complexity

Cons

- Nothing notable

Rating

The plugin has a rating of 4.7 out of 5 stars and has been downloaded over 3 million times.

Conclusion

This may just be the SEO plugin that takes the crown from the longtime favorite, All in One SEO Pack. It does practically everything you could ever want an SEO plugin to do in a way that's easy to understand and use. Just about any WordPress site could benefit from this plugin.

Alternate Options

All in One SEO Pack

`http://wordpress.org/extend/plugins/all-in-one-seo-pack/`

– Probably the most popular free SEO plugin ever with over 13 million downloads. It's simple, effective, and still considered the SEO plugin standard by some. It does have a 3.8-star rating, though, as some people have had minor problems with it.

Headspace2 SEO

`http://wordpress.org/extend/plugins/headspace2/`

– This is another free SEO plugin. This one lets you easily fine-tune the SEO on your WordPress site. Additionally, it allows you to add Google Analytics, Statcounter, Microsoft Live verification, Yahoo! Site Explorer, and many other neat options.

SEO Rank Reporter

`http://wordpress.org/extend/plugins/seo-rank-reporter/`

– This free SEO plugin works a little differently than the others. What it does is track various keywords that you're targeting on your site and report how you rank for them. (This is *much* easier than checking manually.) Since many SEO plugins lack this functionality, it makes a great companion for them.

SEO Smart Links

Price

Original Version – Free

Personal Version - $79

Professional Version - $149

Business Version - $299

Description

SEO Smart Links makes it easy to interlink your web content using your selected keywords. It also allows you to set a "no-follow" attribute to certain links and open them in a new window or tab. Interlinking like this is great for SEO and the no-follow option is great for linking to affiliate offers.

SEO Smart Links

`http://wordpress.org/extend/plugins/seo-automatic-links/`

Pros

- Makes interlinking much less tedious
- Can give a good SEO boost
- Great for affiliate sites that need no-follow links
- Free updates

Cons

- Premium versions are very expensive for what they do
- Bug fixes are almost exclusively limited to the paid versions

Rating

The free version is rated at 3.9 out of 5 stars and has been downloaded over 600,000 times. The paid versions have been downloaded over 300,000 times.

Conclusion

SEO Smart Links is very good at taking the hassle out of internally linking keywords in your web pages. However, the main drawback is that the premium versions get preferential treatment but may not be worth the price.

Alternate Options

SEO Smart Links+

`http://wordpress.org/extend/plugins/seo-smart-links/`

- Functions exactly the same as SEO Smart Links. It may be the better choice if you find that SEO Smart Links has bugs or compatibility issues. This plugin is free and rated at 4 out of 5 stars.

Automatic SEO Links

`http://wordpress.org/extend/plugins/automatic-seo-links/`

– This free plugin is very broad in scope. It will take words and link them to whatever you want; however, it will do this every single time the selected word appears on your site. This is only useful in certain scenarios, as you can imagine.

Vulcan Links to Keywords

`http://wordpress.org/extend/plugins/link-to-words-in-posts/`

– This plugin is like the one above, only it links all the selected keywords in a single post, giving you a bit more control over what you're doing. On the other hand, this also means you'll have to do this for every post or page on your site.

Outbound Link Manager

`http://wordpress.org/extend/plugins/outbound-link-manager/`

– Want to just regulate your outbound links? This free plugin can help. It allows you to regulate no-follow attributes, update tag and anchor text, and remove links altogether if you need to. Best of all, it allows you to do this in bulk across the entire site if you want.

SEO Friendly Images

Price

Free

Description

When it comes to on-page SEO, many people forget how important it is to make sure the images are optimized. This plugin makes optimizing your images very easy by allowing you to add alt and title attributes to them. This gives them a good SEO boost to help you rank higher.

SEO Friendly Images

`http://wordpress.org/extend/plugins/seo-image/`

Pros

- Very easy to use
- Can add alt/title tags automatically or according to the options you select
- Makes images useful for SEO purposes

Cons

- Nothing notable

Rating

SEO Friendly Images has a rating of 4 out of 5 stars and has been downloaded over 800,000 times.

Conclusion

It is important to make your images work toward your overall SEO goals, and this plugin gets the job done. With no notable flaws or complaints from users, this may be the best plugin of its kind available.

Alternate Options

SEO Image Renamer

`http://wordpress.org/extend/plugins/seo-image-renamer/`

– A free plugin designed to rename images after they've been uploaded to the Word-Press media gallery. Has a three-star rating; people seem to either love this plugin or hate it.

WP Image SEO

`http://wordpress.org/extend/plugins/wp-image-seo/`

– Another free plugin that changes your images' title and alt tags to give you an SEO boost. However, this plugin is rated at one star, and people have had trouble getting it to work.

WordPress Flash Tag Cloud

Price

Free

Description

When it comes to SEO, some people say that installing a tag cloud is a big help. Others say it doesn't matter. And still others say it can hurt your ranking. If you do want to install a tag cloud, this plugin lets you do it with style, utilizing fancy Flash animation.

WordPress Flash Cloud

`http://wordpress.org/extend/plugins/wp-flashflyingtags/`

Pros

- Looks cool
- Functions as a tag cloud should

Cons

- Can be distracting

Rating

WordPress Flash Tag Cloud has a rating of 4.2 out of 5 stars.

Conclusion

If you want a tag cloud on your site and you want it to look cool, this is the plugin for you. However, a tag cloud serves no purpose to the visitor whatsoever; it's really only for the search crawlers. There is no practical reason to draw attention to your tag cloud.

Alternate Options

SEO Tag Cloud Widget

```
http://wordpress.org/extend/plugins/seo-tag-cloud/
```

– This is another free plugin that puts a tag cloud on your site. This one isn't as flashy as the one above, so it may be better for those of you who don't want your tag cloud to stick out. It also has an optimized HTML markup.

Fast Category Cloud

```
http://wordpress.org/extend/plugins/fast-category-cloud-
wordpress-plugin/
```

– This is another cloud generator, only this one is for categories, not tags. It gives you several display options, such as color fading, shown post counts, limited categories, and more. It also has a cache option to ensure that it doesn't affect the load time of your site.

SEO Title Tag

Price

Free

Description

Title tags are probably the most important on-page SEO factor. The problem is that post titles should be short and catchy, making it hard to incorporate the proper keyword phrases. SEO Title Tag allows you to override the title tags for your posts, pages, categories, and pretty much any title tag on your entire site, and replace them with SEO-optimized tags while keeping your original titles. In other words, it lets you please both the search engines and your visitors, having the best of both worlds.

SEO Title Tag

`http://wordpress.org/extend/plugins/seo-title-tag/`

Pros

- Excellent for on-page SEO
- Very quick and easy to use
- Can edit titles on a very large scale

Cons

- Hasn't been updated since 2009
- May suffer from compatibility issues in the future if it isn't updated

Rating

3.8 out of 5 stars, with over 300,000 downloads

Conclusion

This is a great plugin that provides a much needed function: optimizing your title tags. Not only that, it also allows you to do so in a very convenient and hassle-free manner. The only drawback is that the creator seems to have abandoned the plugin, making it susceptible to issues of compatibility as new WordPress versions are released. This great plugin may eventually become unusable, which is a shame, since there aren't many options available for this sort of thing.

Alternate Options

<u>Category SEO Meta Tags</u>

```
http://wordpress.org/extend/plugins/category-seo-meta-tags/
```

– This is a much narrower plugin that allows you to edit your category tags to make them more SEO-friendly. It is good at what it does, but it doesn't really do much overall.

<u>AutoSEO</u>

http://wordpress.org/extend/plugins/auto-seo/

– This free plugin allows you to edit your title tags manually across your site all in one go, much like SEO Title Tag. It is also highly customizable and claims to be extremely fast. So far, though, only just over 6,000 people have downloaded it, so it is relatively untested as far as plugins go.

Social Share Plugins

Something that is steadily becoming more important for SEO these days is the presence of social indicators, such as "likes" on Facebook and "+1's" on Google+. Because of this, it is a great idea to have social share buttons on your site, which you can do using plugins.

Digg Digg

Price

Free

Description

Digg Digg is a plugin that ads a social share bar to your WordPress site. The cool thing about it is that it can be set to display on every page, and can even be made to scroll with the screen so it is always visible. It features buttons for many popular social media sites, like Facebook, Twitter, Reddit, StumbleUpon, and many more.

Digg Digg

```
http://wordpress.org/extend/plugins/digg-digg/
```

Pros

- Has plenty of social media buttons to choose from
- Highly visible, which attracts more clicks
- Very customizable, allowing you to set it up how you want

Cons

- Some people claim that it slows down their websites' load times

Rating

This plugin has a rating of 3.5 out of 5 stars, with over 500,000 downloads.

Conclusion

Digg Digg makes it very easy to get the social signals you need for SEO purposes in a way that doesn't force you to manually put social buttons all over your site. Though a few people have said it slows down their website, most have had no problem with it, and the developer has endeavored to make it so that the plugin doesn't affect load times. If there is a problem, they're working on it.

Alternate Options

AA's Dig Dig Alternative

```
http://wordpress.org/extend/plugins/aas-digg-digg-
alternative/
```

– This plugin is a direct competitor to Digg Digg, as the name suggests. It has much of the same functionality, only it claims to also have faster load times, cleaner code, less code overall, and be easy to customize. It has a rating of 4.8 out of 5 stars but only around 3,600 downloads.

Social Box

```
http://codecanyon.net/item/socialbox-social-wordpress-
widget/627127
```

– This plugin comes in the form of a widget that you can place in your sidebar. Instead of focusing on "likes" and "+1's," it encourages people to actively subscribe to your social media accounts, such as following you on Twitter or subscribing to you on YouTube. It also shows your current subscriber count as well. This doesn't give you immediate SEO juice, but it could be useful in the long run if you're trying to get more followers/subscribers. Social Box costs $6 for the regular license and $30 for the extended license.

Slick Social Share Buttons

```
http://wordpress.org/extend/plugins/slick-social-share-
buttons/
```

– This free plugin is very similar to Dig Dig. It does, however, have the additional option to open and close the social box as well as an "auto-close" feature that some visitors to your site may like if they find a floating social bar obnoxious. Slick Social Share Buttons has a rating of 4.4 out of 5 stars and is a favorite of many bloggers.

Social Media Tabs

`http://wordpress.org/extend/plugins/social-media-tabs/`

– This plugin allows you to create widgets with social media tabs as well as snippets from your various social media feeds, like tweets and Facebook posts. Social Media Tabs is a free plugin and rated at 4.6 out of 5 stars.

Social Network Tabs

`http://codecanyon.net/item/social-network-tabs-for-wordpress/1982987`

– It functions much like Social Media Tabs, in that it can display feeds in addition to social buttons, but it has many more options. With over 17 social networks to choose from and over 70 feed options, this is an exceptional social tab plugin. Additionally, the tab box can be displayed on any edge of your browser, or you can place slide-out tabs in your actual content, giving you plenty of ways to work with this plugin. Social Network Tabs is a great deal, at only $12 for a regular license.

WordPress Social Share Buttons

`http://codecanyon.net/item/wordpress-social-share-buttons/2927356`

– A simple, straightforward social share plugin. This one allows you to place social share buttons in multiple locations across your site, using a stylish floating panel. It also has anti-spam capabilities and has been optimized to keep it from overlapping your content on mobile devices. WordPress Social Share Buttons costs $8 for a regular license.

FB Page Integrator
Price

Regular License - $8

Extended License - $40

Description

If you like building Facebook pages to work closely with your main website, this plugin can be a big help. It allows you to edit Facebook fan pages using WordPress, which can save a lot of time.

FB Page Integrator

```
http://codecanyon.net/item/fb-page-integrator-wordpress-
plugin/308746
```

Pros

- Can help you save time if you're using a Facebook page in conjunction with your main website
- Once set up, it's easy to use

Cons

- Must be frequently updated to keep up with Facebook's changes
- Setup can be complicated, since the instructions are vague.

Rating

This plugin currently has a buyer rating of 4 out of 5 stars.

Conclusion

FB Page Integrator is great at what it does: allowing you to work on your Facebook fan page from your website's interface. The only issue is that the instructions to get it set up are extremely vague, which may cause some to get lost. Also, since this plugin works closely with Facebook, it tends to need to be updated whenever Facebook is updated. Fortunately, so far the developer has been really good about putting out updates.

Alternate Options

Facebook Walleria

```
http://codecanyon.net/item/facebook-walleria-wordpress-
plugin/634775
```

– Functions much like FB Page Integrator but also allows you to embed lots of Facebook content directly into your site. This includes albums, photos, feeds, comments, videos, and more. Even better is the fact that it allows you to update all of this, and even interact with your fans directly, from your website. While this plugin may be slightly better than FB Page Integrator, it also costs more: $14 for the regular license and $70 for the extended.

Facebook Fan Page

```
http://wordpress.org/extend/plugins/facebook-fan-page/
```

– This free plugin doesn't function like FB Page Integrator, but it does allow you to install a Facebook fan page widget on your site. It includes wall posts and user comments from your fan page, as well as the ability for people to "like" your content. It also displays photos of featured fans.

Facebook AWD All in One

```
http://wordpress.org/extend/plugins/facebook-awd/
```

– This plugin is a greatly scaled down version of Facebook Walleria and FB Page Integrator that's available for free. It still has many useful options, such as content publishing from your website, "like" buttons, an activity box, and more. It's rated at 4.3 out of 5 stars and has been downloaded over 100,000 times.

WordPress Like Locker

Price

Regular License - $7

Extended License not available

Description

This plugin is somewhat controversial, as it "locks" selected content on your website and forces the viewer to "like" it (using Facebook) to unlock it. This can be a double-edged sword; you could get a lot of likes this way if you have compelling content, or it could have people click away from your site and increase your bounce rate, which is bad for SEO. If you're going to use this plugin, it is recommended that you offer a good amount of compelling content and only lock selected parts after you've got your visitors hooked.

WordPress Like Locker

```
http://codecanyon.net/item/wordpress-like-locker-like-to-
read-plugin/166051
```

Pros

- Very easy to install and use
- Can get you lots of likes

Cons

- Effectiveness of the plugin is contingent on how you use it
- Can work against you if used improperly

Rating

This plugin has a buyer rating of 4 out of 5 stars.

Conclusion

This plugin could be extremely effective if you take the time to use it correctly. For example, you could write a compelling blog post and promise something interesting in the final paragraph, which you lock using the plugin. Or, if you're running a website that's more of a store, you could use it to lock discount codes or coupons. However, many people may be wary of liking something they haven't seen yet, and may click away from your site if you don't give them a good reason to click the like button. Use with discretion.

Alternate Options

Facebook Like Content Locker

```
http://wordpress.org/extend/plugins/facebook-like-content-locker/
```

– This free plugin is essentially a simpler version of WordPress Like Locker. Rather than allowing you to select what you want to lock, it locks your entire blog. As you can imagine, the effectiveness is greatly diminished. That's probably why this plugin has only a 1.3 star rating, out of 5.

Social Locker for WordPress

```
http://codecanyon.net/item/social-locker-for-wordpress/3667715
```

– Functions basically the same as Facebook Like Locker, allowing you to lock parts of your content and forcing visitors to use social buttons to unlock it. The difference is that this one allows visitors to unlock the content using Facebook, Twitter, or Google+. It also comes with built-in analytics tools and is highly customizable. Social Locker for WordPress costs $21 for the regular license and $105 for the developer license, so it's a little on the expensive side.

Social Video Locker –

```
http://codecanyon.net/item/social-video-locker-for-wordpress/2861710
```

This plugin allows you to lock videos and force visitors to share them on Facebook, Google+, Twitter, or LinkedIn before watching. It works with both YouTube and Vimeo videos and comes with a variety of options, such as the ability to allow visitors to unlock all videos on your site by unlocking one, or the ability to put a timer on videos, forcing visitors to have to press social buttons multiple times to view the entire thing. Social Video Locker costs $20 for a standard license and has a 5 out of 5 star rating.

Security Plugins

Now we're going to go over plugins that help make your WordPress sites more secure. Preventing things like hackers, viruses, and spam is very important. Some of you may recognize a few of these from my other book, <u>WordPress Security</u>, which you should check out for more information on how you can keep your site safe from a variety of threats.

Security Ninja

Price

Regular License – $10

Extended License - $50

Description

Security Ninja is the #1 top-selling security plugin on CodeCanyon for a reason. It performs over 31 security tests, including brute force tests, one of the most common hacking techniques. It also checks your site for other threats including malicious code, exploits, and more.

Security Ninja

```
http://codecanyon.net/item/security-ninja/577696
```

Pros

- Very comprehensive all-in-one security plugin
- Easy to use and understand, even for newbies
- Their website allows you to log in and test the plugin

Cons

- Designed to work with other plugins, such as Core Scanner, Scheduled Scanner, and Login Ninja, which must be purchased separately

Rating

Five stars out of five, with ratings from over 200 buyers. This is a very popular plugin.

Conclusion

Security Ninja is a great plugin for any website, taking care of multiple security tasks in an easy-to-understand manner. The only drawback is that the add-ons to enhance its use must be purchased individually. Whether or not they're worth it is up to you.

Alternate Options

Bulletproof Security

`http://wordpress.org/extend/plugins/bulletproof-security/`

– This free plugin packs in a lot of functionality to protect your site against attacks. It includes protection against XXS, RFI, Base64, Code Injections, and much more. It also protects your vital .htaccess files. While this plugin is fast and easy to use, it can be a bit harder to understand due to the hacker jargon used. Even so, it is very popular, with a 4.7 out of 5 star rating and over 450,000 downloads.

Ultimate Security Checker

`http://wordpress.org/extend/plugins/ultimate-security-checker/`

– This is a free plugin that scans your WordPress site and gives it a security rating based on various parameters. The only drawback is that it doesn't actually fix vulnerabilities detected in your system. Still, it's very newbie-friendly and can give you an idea of how secure your site is.

Exploit Scanner

`http://wordpress.org/extend/plugins/exploit-scanner/`

Works much like Ultimate Security Checker and also scans plugins for malicious code as well. However, it also doesn't actually fix any detected exploits. This plugin is free and has been downloaded over 400,000 times.

WordPress Sentinel

`http://wordpress.org/extend/plugins/wordpress-sentinel/`

– A free plugin that watches over your files, particularly your admin files, and notifies you of any changes. This is a great defense against hackers who may attempt to insert malicious code into themes, plugins, or other files.

WP Email Guard

`http://wordpress.org/extend/plugins/wp-email-guard/`

– Having your site crawled by spammers is bad news, especially if they get a hold of your email address. This free plugin safeguards any mention of your email address on your site from being scraped and spammed. Extremely useful, but hasn't been updated since 2009.

Email Obfuscate Shortcode

```
http://wordpress.org/extend/plugins/email-obfuscate-
shortcode/
```

– Provides shortcode to keep your email address from being scraped by spammers. This free plugin has been updated for WordPress 3.5.

Wordfence

Price

Free

Description

This security plugin has some unique features, so it deserves an extended review. What sets Wordfence apart from the pack is the fact that not only does it detect threats, but it can also repair any of your core, theme, and plugin files that may be infected or corrupted. This is the only WordPress security plugin capable of this at this time.

Wordfence

`http://wordpress.org/extend/plugins/wordfence/`

Pros

- Can scan multiple sites from one control panel a real time saver if you have more than one site
- Continuously scans for a huge number of threats, including backdoors, malware, and phishing
- Protects your login from brute-force hackers
- Gives you a real-time view of all traffic on your site.

Cons

- The ability to block countries and do scheduled scans is only available in the paid version.
- Not quite as newbie-friendly due to the huge amount of options and hacker jargon

Rating

Wordfence has a very high rating of 4.8 out of 5 stars and has been downloaded over 200,000 times.

Conclusion

Wordfence may seem a bit complicated at first, but the fact that it can actively fix certain security problems makes it a great plugin, especially since it is free. Also, the fact that it can scan multiple sites from one control panel is a huge plus for anyone with more than one site.

Alternate Options

WordPress File Monitor

`http://wordpress.org/extend/plugins/wordpress-file-monitor/`

– Actively monitors your WordPress files and emails you when changes are made. This plugin is free, but hasn't been updated since 2010. If it isn't updated again, it may become obsolete.

WP Security Scan

`http://wordpress.org/extend/plugins/wp-security-scan/`

– This is a free plugin that also scans your WordPress site for vulnerabilities and exploits. While it won't fix them, it will suggest actions you can take to correct the problems. Key areas that it helps with include passwords, file permissions, database security, and WordPress admin protection. WP Security Scan is very popular, with over one million downloads, but has a fairly average rating of 3.4 out of 5 stars.

Admin SSL

`http://wordpress.org/extend/plugins/admin-ssl-secure-admin/`

– This plugin uses private SSL to help secure your WordPress admin area and keep it safe from hackers. This can be a bit on the technical side, but it does have installation instructions and a FAQ. Admin SSL is free but hasn't been updated since 2009. It may become obsolete soon.

Theme Authenticity Checker (TAC)

```
http://wordpress.org/extend/plugins/tac/
```

– This is a free plugin that searches the source code of themes you download for malicious code. This is a great choice if you often download new themes to try out.

Antivirus

```
http://wordpress.org/extend/plugins/antivirus/
```

– This clearly named plugin does what you'd expect: it scans your WordPress site daily for viruses and malicious injections. If something suspicious is found, you're notified in your admin area and by email. It supports multiple languages.

AskApache Password Protect

Price

Free

Description

Password hacking is one of the oldest tricks in the book for hackers, and the "brute force" method can be devastating to unprotected WordPress sites. AskApache protects your login using HTTP Basic Authentication or the more secure HTTP Digest Authentication. It also has anti-spam capabilities and can protect against other common exploits.

AskApache Password Protect

```
http://wordpress.org/extend/plugins/askapache-password-
protect/
```

Pros

- Great for password protection
- Various extra options and capabilities

Cons

- Hasn't been updated since 2010
- If your web host isn't Apache, it won't protect your .htaccess files

Conclusion

AskApache is great for password protection, which is important since that is what many hackers will target first. The main drawback is the lack of recent support and the fact that your .htaccess files won't be protected unless your site is hosted with Apache. Still, .htaccess protection isn't the main purpose of this plugin anyway, and there are other plugins that can take care of that.

Alternate Options

Login Security Solution

`http://wordpress.org/extend/plugins/login-security-solution/`

– This is a free plugin that has a variety of handy features. In addition to protecting against brute force password hacking, it also tracks usernames, IP addresses, and passwords. It also checks login failures for these factors, slowing down response times when multiple attempts are made, which frustrates would-be hackers.

One-Time Password

`http://wordpress.org/extend/plugins/one-time-password/`

– This plugin is designed to give your login info an extra layer of protection in environments like shared Internet connections at cafés and other public places. It allows you to log in using passwords that only work once. This way, if your password is stolen by a keylogger or other underhanded method, it won't work again. It may seem slightly inconvenient to do it this way, but if you're constantly using a shared connection, it could prevent you from having your password stolen and your account compromised.

SI CAPTCHA Anti-Spam

Price

Free

Description

Protecting a WordPress site against spam is very important if you allow visitors to comment. Bots will spam you relentlessly if you don't take measures to stop them. This plugin not only protects your comments from spam, but also guards your registration, lost password, and login systems for extra security. It allows trackbacks and pingbacks, and also supports 18 different languages.

SI CAPTCHA Anti-Spam

```
http://wordpress.org/extend/plugins/si-captcha-for-
wordpress/
```

Pros

- Provides good anti-spam protection using CAPTCHA
- Protects more than just your comments section
- Great for deterring bots
- Supports multiple languages

Cons

- Several people report spam getting through to their site anyway

Rating

This plugin is rated at 3.8 out of 5 stars, with nearly 1.5 million downloads.

Conclusion

This plugin is great for protecting your comments against spam, along with other critical areas that bots will try to get into, such as the registration screen. Despite its popularity, some have claimed that spam still gets through sometimes, though they are in the minority.

Alternate Options

<u>Akismet</u> –

`http://wordpress.org/extend/plugins/akismet/`

By far the most popular anti-spam plugin for WordPress, though that may have to do with the fact that it comes preloaded on every WordPress installation. Akismet's biggest drawbacks are that it only works for comments and that you have to sign up to their site to get an API key to make it work; it no longer works automatically. Even worse is the fact that if you make any money from your website, Akismet requires you to pay a subscription fee. Still, many people consider it to be the anti-spam standard.

<u>Antispam Bee</u>

`http://wordpress.org/extend/plugins/antispam-bee/`

– This free plugin is considered by many to be the best alternative to Akismet and actually has more functionality and options. The biggest drawback here is that it is in German, which may alienate people who don't speak that language. However, you can enter the following URL into your browser to get a full review of the plugin in English, with a listing of all of its features to help you decide if Antispam Bee is for you.

`http://www.mydigitallife.info/antispam-bee-review-best-free-akismet-alternative-for-wordpress/`

WP-DBManager

Price

Free

Description

No security system is 100% guaranteed to defend against any and all hacking attempts. This makes it very important to back up your data, so if you do get hacked, you won't lose everything. WP-DBManager does this and much more, giving you plenty of database management options to work with, including optimization, repair, back up, restore, delete files, drop/empty tables, and run selected queries.

WP-DBManager

`http://wordpress.org/extend/plugins/wp-dbmanager/`

Pros

- Very comprehensive database management plugin
- Supports automatic scheduling for various tasks

Cons

- Some options may be hard for newbies to understand

Rating

WP-DBManager has a rating of 3.9 out of 5 stars and has been downloaded over 750,000 times.

Conclusion

One of the best free database management plugins around. It backs up your data to keep it safe, and performs a number of other handy tasks. However, some of the more advanced options may be a bit technically complex for those not experienced with database management.

Alternate Options

WP-DB-Backup

```
http://wordpress.org/extend/plugins/wp-db-backup/
```

– A very simple and straightforward free plugin that allows you to back up your data. Extremely popular, with over 1.5 million downloads, but hasn't been updated since 2010. Due to this, it may become obsolete in the future.

Simple Backup

```
http://codecanyon.net/item/simple-backup/104945
```

– This is another very straightforward plugin. This one can also be scheduled to perform backups automatically using cron, though that may be a bit complicated for those not technically inclined. The regular license costs $8, while the extended one costs $40.

VaultPress

```
http://vaultpress.com/
```

– This is *not* a plugin, but it may just be the most comprehensive and complete security system for WordPress available. VaultPress is a subscription-based service, starting at $5 a month per site, that performs a variety of security functions like real-time database backup, automatic site restoration, daily security scans, and review/repair of security threats, just to name a few.

Themes for Stores and Affiliate Sites

When choosing a theme for a store or affiliate site, what you need can vary depending on the type of store or site you're building. For example, an Amazon affiliate store would be set up differently than a store that sells health supplements and related products. Sites like these need to have a strong visual element, especially on the main page. Here are a few themes that are great for stores and affiliate sites.

Affiliate Theme 2.0

Price

Standard Package – $77

Premium Package – $97

Deluxe Package – $147

Description

Affiliate Theme 2.0 is a simple WordPress theme designed specifically for affiliate sites. The main page is very clean, featuring a strong visual element and limited navigation options that help push potential customers where you want them to go. Sidebar and widget options are restricted to internal pages and posts, allowing easy navigation for viewers once they've clicked on a product or offer.

The main benefit is probably the selection of various skins for the site, allowing you to customize it to fit what you're selling. Some examples of included skins are Amazon, travel, dating, and web hosting.

The Standard Package is $77 and comes with five skins, six unique template pages, and tutorials/support. It also has 10 pre-made niche header graphics included as a bonus. Best of all, it can be used on an unlimited number of sites with no developer's license needed.

The Premium Package costs a bit more, but comes with 50 niche headers. The Deluxe Package is the same as the Premium Package, but comes with installation, which is honestly kind of unnecessary; installing a theme is easy.

Afilliate Theme 2.0

`http://www.affiliatetheme.net/`

Pros

- Very sharp, clean look
- Very good use of images on the main page
- Includes several skins to use
- Setup wizard makes getting started easy
- The Marketplace allows for the purchase of additional skins/services

- The Marketplace also allows you to sell skins and services
- Support and tutorials are included at no extra charge

Cons

- May be a bit too simplistic for some people
- Deluxe Package doesn't really justify its price

Conclusion

Overall, Affiliate Theme 2.0 is a very solid affiliate theme that allows you to customize it with various skins while still maintaining the simple and sharp look of the site. It's easy to use, and support and tutorials are readily available if you need them. On top of this, the Marketplace has plenty of stuff for you to buy and sell, making this a very good deal for $77. Web developers will love the fact that they don't have to pay extra for a developer's license.

InReview

Price

$39.

As of this writing, this price not only gets you this theme, but the other 80 themes from Elegant as well, which is an incredible bargain.

Description

Making a review website to sell products used to be a lot of work. Most people would take a standard blog template and add in the graphics, pictures, and other necessary bells and whistles manually. InReview, made by prominent theme designers Elegant Themes, makes creating a review website much easier.

The site has the standard navigation options at the top, beneath the header, and then allows a space for a message of your choice. This is a great place to advertise a sale, discount, or other special promotion because it will get a lot of attention there. Below that, you'll find a featured item area that can be configured to rotate among several products; once again, this makes for a great opportunity to showcase special offers and hot deals.

Just below all this comes the real meat of the theme: tons of product placements. On the left/center, you can have pictures showcasing several products with short snippets from the reviews as well as their star ratings. In the right-hand sidebar, you can have smaller product pictures with ratings as well, grouped using widgets like "Top Editor-Rated Products," "Top User-Rated Products," and others. Other widgets displaying recent comments/posts are also available.

InReview

`http://www.elegantthemes.com/gallery/inreview/`

Pros

- Constantly being updated by Elegant Themes for best performance
- Compatible with all major browsers
- Convenient star rating system for both you and your users to use
- Designed for easy affiliate integration
- Complete localization for easy translation for foreign customers
- Comes in five unique colors

- Exceptional support in case you need help
- Plenty of theme options, shortcodes, page templates, and more
- Eighty themes for the price of one

Cons

- Main page can become cluttered if you don't know what you're doing
- Intelligent use of images and image placement will be needed to use this theme effectively

Conclusion

InReview is an amazing template for review-style stores and sites, taking a lot of the work out of the process. The star system allows you to rate products across various categories as well as give them an overall rating. It also allows users to give ratings in the comments section, encouraging user participation. Additionally, it allows for easy creation of "buy it now" buttons that can be given a call-to-action of your choice.

The amount of options you get is very impressive, and the main page does a great job of showcasing your products and their ratings, which is a surefire way to get people clicking on them. The only real issue is that the main page can become cluttered and messy if you don't know what you're doing. Overall, though, InReview can save you a lot of time and effort when setting up a review site.

Also, eighty themes for the price of one is one of the best deals I've ever seen. However, I have no way of knowing how long this offer will last.

ProReview Theme

Price:

Single Site License - $37

Multi-Site License - $69

Developer License - $119

Description

ProReview claims to be the best review theme online, and it could be right about that. Optimized for two of the most popular affiliate programs around, Amazon and ClickBank, this theme has a lot to offer. The easy-to-use options panel offers a great deal of control and the ability to customize the theme to your liking.

ProReview features a rather standard header and top navigation area and has a prominent slider that can feature multiple products. The slider also has a little bar on the right, showcasing three additional products of your choice. This is a great way to show off your best-sellers and really maximize your profits. Below this, you can add a little "welcome to the site" blurb if you want before you get into the product listings.

The product listings are done very well; they're located on the left/center with large pictures, a star rating, and a review snippet. Additionally, it has a "Visit Site Now" button that takes visitors directly to the offer using your affiliate link. Since the ultimate purpose of a review site is to get people to the main website to buy the offer, this is a huge plus for this theme. You can also insert banner advertisements between the review listings on the main page if you feel the need, though this could be a distraction.

The right sidebar has plenty of options, too. You can insert widgets displaying top-rated products, social media widgets to help spread the word about your site, and even a product-review video if you want. You also have the option for traditional blog-style posts on the main page but, once again, that could end up being a distraction for potential customers.

The product review pages themselves look great, featuring attractive images, star ratings, and a "Visit Site Now" button right up at the top; a very smart move. Comments also allow visitors to add their own star ratings.

ProReview Theme

`http://proreviewtheme.com/`

Pros

- Fits a lot of information on the main page without seeming cluttered
- Star-rating system is convenient to use
- Sidebar has lots of great options
- Easy to place banner ads if you want to
- Works great with video
- Easy navigation

Cons

- The overall design is set up like a traditional blog, which some may consider old-fashioned
- Adding too many features like banner ads and blog posts could distract customers from the products

Conclusion

ProReview is a very solid review theme, especially as it was developed specifically for the Amazon and ClickBank affiliate programs. However, it would also be a good theme for practically any review site you could imagine. It has plenty of options to really make your site unique while still looking sleek and attractive.

The main benefit to this theme is how it manages to pack in a ton of useful info about various products on the main page without overwhelming a potential customer. The inclusion of ads and blog posts could work against you, though, if you decide to use them.

Magazine Basic

Price

Free

Description

This WordPress theme is, as its name says, very basic. However, it is also very customizable and offers a lot of different layout options, including the placement of your sidebars, the width/height of the theme, and color options. Getting this theme to look good for an affiliate/review site will take some work, but it is so versatile that it can accommodate practically any site you could ever want to make.

For example, you can place your main content in the middle and have two sidebars, or just have a single sidebar and let your content take up a larger area. You can also add sliders, special headers and footers, and much more. There is really a lot you can do with this theme.

Magazine Basic

`http://themes.bavotasan.com/2008/magazine-basic/`

Pros

- Versatile
- Simple and attractive
- Easy to use
- Plenty of places for ad placement
- Free

Cons

- Will take some work to get set up
- You'll need to have at least some knowledge of web development to make your site look attractive
- Design is very simple looking

Conclusion

Magazine Basic is an excellent all-purpose theme that can be used for just about anything, including affiliate/review sites. The base design has very few distractions for potential customers, but looks somewhat dated. The theme is so versatile that you're going to have to do some work to get it to look how you want, and it will take some web design know-how to do that. If you're familiar with web design and want a free theme that you can do all kinds of things with, this is a good choice.

Zenshop

Price

Free

Description

Zenshop is a theme specifically designed to work with the e-commerce plugin Cart66, which I'll go over later. The theme looks very sleek and professional, considering it is free, and has a lot of potential for various types of affiliate/review sites as well as other forms of e-commerce.

It doesn't have much of a header, sacrificing that space in order to fit more important things "above the fold," like the large, bold product slider and the product listings below it. Those product listings are displayed on the main page in a grid-like fashion with big, prominent images. There are no star ratings or review snippets, only a link for more information and the price.

The product review pages also have massive images up top and a simple yet stylish look. The sidebar contains various widgets, such as a shopping cart recap, categories, ads, etc. There are a lot of options to work with here.

Zenshop

`http://www.fabthemes.com/zenshop/`

Pros

- Visually impressive
- Simple layout won't overwhelm potential customers
- Plenty of sidebar options
- Very visually oriented
- Add-to-cart button
- Plenty of footer options

Cons

- No fancy features, like a star-rating system

- Simple layout can look plain and unexciting

Rating

Zenshop has a rating of 4.35 on FabThemes.

Conclusion

In the end, Zenshop is a visually striking theme that gets the job done. The use of large images is definitely an eye-catcher, but there are no bells and whistles to really take the theme to the next level. The simplistic look has both positive and negative qualities, but still manages to be attractive. Overall, this theme is great if you're looking for something free; just don't expect a lot of neat features and options to play around with.

Plugins for Stores and Affiliate Sites

There are many great plugins for stores and affiliate sites. Some transform your theme into a virtual storefront, while others add much-needed functionality like a shopping cart.

MaxBlogPress Affiliate Ninja
Price

Single-Site License - $37

Developer License - $97

Description

This plugin functions as a link tracker, allowing you to obtain accurate stats so that you can better optimize your affiliate site. However, it does much more than that. MaxBlogPress Affiliate Ninja also allows you to create redirect links, cloak your links, manage links by groups, create no-follow links, turn your keywords into links, and more. When it comes to configuring your affiliate links, this plugin does it all.

MaxBlogPress Affiliate Ninja

`http://mbpninjaaffiliate.com/ninja-trial-2.php`

Pros

- Lots of options
- Easy-to-use dashboard with stat tracking
- Helps to prevent affiliate theft
- A big time-saver
- A big help when it comes to split testing anchor text
- Smart caching system keeps your site running smoothly

Cons

- It is completely oriented around affiliate links and offers no other features.

Rating

None available

Conclusion

If you want more control over your affiliate links, this plugin has what you need. Used correctly, it can help you improve conversion rates and the amount of money you make by allowing you to optimize your links based on accurate data. It has a lot of features, but they all have to do with links and nothing else.

Alternate Options

Pretty Link Lite

`http://wordpress.org/extend/plugins/pretty-link/`

– This free plugin offers quite a bit of functionality. Its main purpose is to shorten links, much like tinyurl.com, only it uses your own domain to do it. It also offers link tracking both on your site and anywhere you use the link-shortening function. Pretty Link Lite is currently rated at 4.1 out of 5 stars and has been downloaded close to 600,000 times.

Amazon Affiliate Link Localizer

`http://wordpress.org/extend/plugins/amazon-affiliate-link-localizer/`

– This free plugin is a major time-saver for anyone with an Amazon store. It automatically changes any link to Amazon into your affiliate link so you don't have to do it manually over and over again. It also directs customers to the Amazon store appropriate for their region; for instance, if you get a customer from the UK, it will direct them to the UK Amazon site. This is a great way to keep from losing international sales.

Amazon Link

`http://wordpress.org/extend/plugins/amazon-link/`

– Very similar to Amazon Affiliate Link Localizer, this plugin has a few extra features, including a search tool, affiliate tracking IDs, and a caching system to keep your site running smoothly. It's also free and has a rating of 3.7 out of 5 stars.

Affiliate Links Manager

`http://wordpress.org/extend/plugins/affiliate-links-manager/`

– This free plugin includes a few essential functions: affiliate link tracking via Google Analytics, link redirects, and server load reduction.

Affiliate Link Cloaker

`http://wordpress.org/extend/plugins/alc/`

– Very simple free plugin that cloaks links. It can also be configured to work manually or automatically. Good for preventing affiliate theft.

attentionGrabber

Price

Regular License - $12

No Extended License Available

Description

This plugin displays an eye-catching notification bar on your website. This is very simple, but useful; it's great for promoting sales, discounts, and other special offers. It has plenty of customization options, animation affects, a click counter, and modules for Facebook likes, Twitter, and Google+. It can also incorporate RSS, ATOM, and Twitter feeds as well.

AttentionGrabber

`http://codecanyon.net/item/attentiongrabber-wordpress-notification-bar/242027`

Pros

- Great way to draw attention to special sales and hot products
- Plenty of ways to customize it so it fits with your theme
- Has many handy features
- Can help increase sales, newsletter signups, and Facebook likes

Cons

- The notification bar looks kind of basic when it could have been more eye-catching.

Rating

This plugin has a 5 out of 5 star rating from over 200 buyers.

Conclusion

Drawing your customers' attention to special deals and other important information is easy with this plugin. It's very simple to use, but has enough options to allow you to customize it to your liking. Extra features like incorporating Facebook likes and Twitter feeds are a really nice touch.

Alternate Choices

EZ Notification Bar

```
http://codecanyon.net/item/ez-notification-bar/2478002
```

– This plugin is like a scaled-down version of attentionGrabber. It is fully customizable and actually a bit more impressive graphically. It is also cheaper at only $5 and fulfills its primary function very well.

WordPress Notification Bar

```
http://wordpress.org/extend/plugins/wordpress-notification-bar/
```

– Very simple notification bar with customizable color and multi-site functionality. Has a rating of 4.9 out of 5 stars. Free.

Duplicator

Price

Free

Description

This plugin allows you to quickly and easily duplicate WordPress sites. If you're creating multiple niche sites that follow the same template and layout, this plugin can save you a lot of time. It also functions as a backup utility.

Duplicator

`http://wordpress.org/extend/plugins/duplicator/`

Pros

- Makes it very easy to clone sites
- Huge time-saver
- Can be used to back up sites in case you get hacked
- Works in only three steps

Cons

- Takes a bit of technical know-how to use

Rating

4.8 out of 5 stars.

Conclusion

This plugin is handy when you want to make multiple sites fast, which is a common strategy among those involved in e-commerce. The only downside is that a certain level of technical knowledge is needed to use it.

Alternate Choices

NS Cloner

`http://wordpress.org/extend/plugins/ns-cloner-site-copier/`

– This website cloner is meant to work with WordPress Multisite, not single installations. Easy to use and free. It has a rating of 5 out of 5 stars, but only two ratings so far.

XCloner

`http://wordpress.org/extend/plugins/xcloner-backup-and-restore/`

– This is an up-and-coming free plugin that allows you to back up your files and database. Still takes some technical know-how to use. It has a score of 4.4 out of 5 stars and has been downloaded close to 150,000 times.

ReviewAZON Pro 2.0

Price

$79

Description

One of the most well-known Amazon store plugins, ReviewAZON 2.0 has a ton of functionality and features. It transforms an ordinary site into an Amazon store quickly and easily. It gives you the ability to use the star rating system, insert affiliate links, insert buy buttons that look just like the ones on Amazon.com, and much more. One of its best features is the fact that it can take info straight from Amazon such as product rating, list price, sale price, customer reviews, and more. And this is just the tip of the iceberg.

ReviewAZON Pro 2.0

`http://reviewazon.com/`

Pros

- Many, many features. Everything you'd need to turn your site into an Amazon store.
- Very easy to use
- Takes out much of the hassle of setting up your own store
- Can turn just about any theme template into a functioning Amazon store
- Includes lifetime updates and access to the members-only support forums.

Cons

- The amount of options available may be overwhelming at first

Rating

None available

Conclusion

The price of $79 isn't exactly cheap, but you do get a ton of value for your money with ReviewAZON 2.0. It has everything you could ever need to turn your site into a fully functional Amazon store. It's also very easy to use, though it can be easy to get overwhelmed by the sheer amount of things you can do with this plugin. This may be the ultimate Amazon store plugin.

Alternate Options

<u>WP Zon Builder</u>

`http://www.wpzonbuilder.com/`

– This is another Amazon store builder with plenty of options. This one features multi-national functionality to help cater to an international audience. This plugin seems geared toward sites that feature more product graphics on the home page. It comes with an unlimited site license for $99.

<u>phpZon Pro</u>

`http://www.phpbay.com/phpzon-pro-wordpress-plugin.html`

– This $79 plugin comes with a lot, including the ability to list a product by ASIN, display product description snippets, display product features, and SEO URL features. The end result looks really good and is great for sites that need to list large numbers of products.

<u>Amazon Reloaded</u>

`http://wordpress.org/extend/plugins/amazon-reloaded-for-wordpress/`

– A free plugin that makes it easy to get both image and text links from Amazon for use in your store. It can be configured to put your affiliate tag in these links automatically, saving you a lot of time. While it may not have the functionality of the paid plugins, it does its job well.

<u>**Affiliate Easel for Amazon**</u>

`http://wordpress.org/extend/plugins/affiliate-easel-for-amazon/`

– This free plugin has a variety of functions, allowing you to quickly and easily get the info you need from Amazon to post on your site. It also supports easy insertion of your affiliate ID. However, at this time it only supports compatibility with the US Amazon store. It has a rating of 2.1 out of 5 stars.

WordPress eStore Plugin

Price

$49.95

Description

WordPress eStore Plugin has a massive number of features for turning your site into a fully functional e-store. It has an integrated shopping cart, affiliate software integration, Amazon S3 integration, product display templates, secure download manager, the ability to create membership sites, and much more. It also comes with a standard multi-site license, which is always great. Included as part of the deal are a bunch of other plugins: Extra eStore Shortcodes, eStore Bulk Item Purchase, and eStore Post Payment Actions, among others.

WordPress eStore Plugin

```
http://www.tipsandtricks-hq.com/wordpress-estore-plugin-
complete-solution-to-sell-digital-products-from-your-
wordpress-blog-securely-1059
```

Pros

- You get a lot for what you pay
- Can be used to create any kind of store and sell any kind of product
- Comes with a multi-site license
- Has squeeze page capabilities for list/newsletter subscription
- Product display template looks very sharp

Cons

- Has so many features that it may take some time to set everything up
- Jack-of-all-trades, master of none

Rating

None available

Conclusion

If you want an all-purpose e-store builder, this is a great plugin. You can use it to build Amazon stores, ClickBank stores, bookstores, wholesale stores, etc. The only issue here is that it isn't optimized for any one type of store. If you're building an

Amazon store or ClickBank store in particular, there may be better plugins for your specific needs. However, at only $49.95, this is still an excellent value and may prove more useful if you want to build many different types of stores, since it comes with a multi-site license.

Alternate Options

<u>Cart66</u>

`https://cart66.com/`

– This popular plugin is great for selling both physical and digital products. It features both Amazon S3 and PayPal integration, making it a great choice for anyone who sells their own products, like e-books, mp3s, or anything else you create on your own. Additionally, it is pre-optimized to work with certain themes, such as ZenShop. It even calculates rates for UPS, USPS, FedEx, and Canadian and Australian shipping. If you want to set up an e-commerce site that isn't an affiliate site, this is a great plugin. Just be aware that the free standard version has fewer features than the pro version, which starts at $89.

<u>Shopp</u>

`https://shopplugin.net/`

– One of the most flexible and versatile e-commerce plugins available. It offers integration with PayPal, Google Wallet, and 2Checkout.com. It also has many add-on integrators, like real-time shipping rates, order fulfillment services, cloud storage, and more. A single site license is $55; a developer license is $299.

<u>Quick Shop</u>

`http://wordpress.org/extend/plugins/quick-shop/`

– This is a free plugin that adds a variety of essential options for e-commerce sites, such as a shopping cart, a checkout page, and multiple product display options. Lacks many of the features of paid plugins, but has the bare minimum needed for a store. Has a rating of 3.7 out of 5 stars and has been downloaded almost 100,000 times.

PG Simple Affiliate Shop

```
http://wordpress.org/extend/plugins/pg-simple-affiliate-
shop/
```

– Allows many handy options, like the ability to attach testimonials, product descriptions, and images. You can customize banners and buy-now buttons, too. This is a free plugin with a 5 out of 5 star rating but only 3 ratings so far.

Responsive Pricing Table – Pure CSS

Price

Regular License - $4

Extended License - $20

Description

Sometimes, certain items or services for sale need special price tables to show different variations and pricing options. This plugin uses CSS and HTML to take care of that, so you don't have to bother uploading images. The interface makes this plugin very easy to use without you having to do actual CSS and HTML coding; it does it for you! It is very flexible and allows you to create a wide variety of pricing tables to fit your needs. It also comes with "yes" and "no" icons to help you differentiate product versions and features.

Responsive Pricing Table – Pure CSS

`http://codecanyon.net/item/-responsive-pricing-table-pure-css/3162267`

Pros

- Easy to use
- Very flexible and customizable
- "Yes" and "no" icons are very convenient
- Pricing tables look sleek and professional
- Animated and non-animated tables available
- 252 total pricing tables

Cons

- This relatively new plugin has only 15 purchases so far, so it hasn't gotten a lot of feedback yet

Rating

None available

Conclusion

Responsive Pricing Table – Pure CSS makes it easy to add pricing tables to your e-commerce website. This is particularly great for sites that sell software and services. It has a ton of options and is very flexible, letting you create a table perfect for your site. However, it is very new and hasn't gotten a lot of feedback yet, making its true performance somewhat unknown. Still, it doesn't cost much.

Alternate Choices

<u>uPricing</u> –

```
http://codecanyon.net/item/upricing-pricing-table-for-
wordpress/145538
```

This is another price table creator for WordPress. While it lacks some of the functionality of Pure CSS, it does have all of the core components, such as multiple templates, customizable fonts/colors, and a live preview feature. It costs $15 for the standard license and $75 for the extended, and has a four-star rating with over 900 purchases.

<u>Price Table</u> –

```
http://wordpress.org/extend/plugins/pricetable/
```

Just like the name of this free plugin, Price Table is basic but functional. It uses CSS3 to allow you to create drag and drop price tables quickly and easily. Nothing fancy here but it gets the job done.

Pricing Table –

`http://wordpress.org/extend/plugins/pricing-table/`

This is another free pricing table plugin with basic functionality. It looks a bit better than Price Table and features slightly more options, such as the ability to highlight a featured column as the best value in the package.

Multipurpose Bookshelf Slider

Price

Regular License - $12

Extended License - $60

Description

The name says it all: this plugin allows you to display product images in an attractive, "bookshelf" style. As you might imagine, this is an excellent plugin for selling e-books and physical books. It also works really well for selling DVDs, CDs, mp3s, comics, or any other product that relies on having a strong, clear visual image. It is meant to display images in gallery style and has been optimized to work with the Woo-Commerce plugin. It can also display videos as well, making it great for product video reviews.

Multipurpose Bookshelf Slider

```
http://codecanyon.net/item/multipurpose-bookshelf-slider-
wordpress-plugin/2228996
```

Pros

- Great for displaying product images in a professional, visually powerful manner
- Easy to use and configure
- Cross-browser compatibility
- Widget and shortcode full setup

Cons

- May not work as well with products like jewelry, pet supplies, etc.
- Virtually useless for selling services

Rating

This plugin has a buyer rating of 5 out of 5 stars.

Conclusion

This plugin can add a distinctive, professional visual element to your e-commerce site. It is easy to use and very functional, but may not be much use for certain types of e-commerce sites. If you're selling books, though, this one is a real winner.

Alternate Options

Image Gallery Reloaded

`http://wordpress.org/extend/plugins/image-gallery-reloaded/`

– Creates a great, yet somewhat generic image gallery for your site. It can be useful for certain categories, or on the home page if your theme lacks an inbuilt gallery. It's fully customizable and features a slide-show function. This plugin is free and has a rating of 3.9 out of 5 stars.

iFrame Images Gallery

`http://wordpress.org/extend/plugins/wp-iframe-images-gallery/`

– Free plugin that creates a very simplistic image gallery scroll bar. Must be scrolled manually using a slider. Nothing fancy, but may be useful in certain situations.

Pinterest Plugin

`http://wordpress.org/extend/plugins/pinterest-plugin/`

– Pinterest is a very popular new social media site that revolves around creating image galleries. This plugin puts the "Pin It" button on selected images on your site, allowing viewers to quickly and easily pin them to their Pinterest galleries, using the alt-code of the image as the default title. This can lead to a lot of great traffic from Pinterest to your website. This plugin is free and is rated at 3.4 out of 5 stars.

CBPress

Price

Free

Description

This plugin allows you to turn your site into a ClickBank store and sell their products as an affiliate. It can import a full marketplace of products and categories, as well as allowing you to fully edit the product information to your liking. You can import from ClickBank category lists, or create your own product lists if you want. In addition to this, you can also add affiliate products from other sources than ClickBank.

CBPress

`http://wordpress.org/extend/plugins/cbpress/`

Pros

- Put ClickBank products on your site quickly and easily
- Allows for plenty of customization
- Allows the promotion of non-ClickBank products as well
- License allows you to use it on multiple sites

Cons

- There have been issues with updates and support
- A few people have reported compatibility issues with WordPress 3.5

Rating

This plugin has a rating of 3.4 out of 5 stars

Conclusion

Overall, this is a good plugin for creating a ClickBank-based affiliate store. It doesn't have quite the number of options or capabilities that Amazon plugins have for Amazon stores, but keep in mind that this plugin is free. Some people have raised concerns about the amount of support that this plugin gets from its developer.

Alternate Choices

CB Storefront

`http://wordpress.org/extend/plugins/cb-storefront/`

– Similar to CBPress, this free plugin allows you to create a ClickBank storefront by presenting ClickBank products using their feed and your affiliate ID. It uses shortcode to insert the product galleries on your website pages, so there is some manual work involved. However, these listings are also self-updating, so once you have it set up, you're good to go.

ClickBank Sale Notification

`http://wordpress.org/extend/plugins/clickbank-sale-notification/`

– Enjoy the feeling of knowing you just made a sale from your store? This plugin sends you an email notification every time you make a sale. It also notifies you of re-bills, refunds, chargebacks, and cancel re-bills. It may be best to create a specific email account just to use with this plugin; you don't want your main email account being flooded if you make a ton of sales. This plugin is free.

Themes for Blogs

Blogging is still probably the number-one way WordPress is used. If you've switched over to WordPress.org from WordPress.com or another free provider, you'll be happy to know that you have a lot of options when it comes to getting a great theme for your blog.

Sahifa

Price

Regular License - $45

Extended License - $2250 (no, that's not a typo!)

Description

Sahifa is an extremely good-looking theme built to accommodate a magazine, news, or blog style. It was designed with mobile capability in mind and features HTML5 functionality. The homepage builder is drag-and–drop, making it very easy to use, even for newbies. It has a ton of options and features, including 30 custom widgets, 70+ shortcodes, 8 page templates, 500+ Google web fonts, unlimited sidebars and unlimited colors. It even has a rating system built in that can use stars, percentages, and more. Other features include an integrated favicon uploader, a logo uploader, custom gravitar uploader, and full screen background options.

As for how it looks, Sahifa is very crisp and professional. The homepage is very image-oriented, making it great for blogs that use a lot of images for their posts. The theme has a large featured image at the top that can function as a slider; below that, you can have a recent posts section, a blog roll, banner ads, and more.

The default main page has a sidebar, allowing you to display such information as social buttons, Facebook widgets, Flickr Widgets, popular posts, etc. All of this is fully customizable (and image heavy, of course), making it look great.

Sahifa

```
http://themeforest.net/item/sahifa-responsive-wordpress-
newsmagazineblog/2819356
```

Pros

- Massive amount of features and options
- Great for a variety of blog types, especially image-oriented ones like news sites
- Highly customizable for a unique look
- Very crisp, clean, and professional-looking
- Easy to use

- Useful features, like the rating system, that you wouldn't expect a blog theme to have

Cons

- The amount of options may be overkill for a simple blog
- Easy to get overwhelmed with the sheer amount of things you can do with this WordPress theme
- Extended license is insanely expensive

Rating

Sahifa has a buyer rating of 5 out of 5 stars from over 200 buyers. It has been purchased close to 2,000 times, making it a very popular paid theme.

Conclusion

I don't think I've ever come across another WordPress theme with the amount of options and features that Sahifa has. There are literally tons of things you can do with it, making it a great choice for practically any blog, and even for review style e-commerce sites, thanks to the ratings system. On top of that, it looks incredible and can give any blog an aura of professionalism. You get a huge amount of value for $45. At the same time, this may be overkill for those who want just a simple blog.

The Style

Price

$39. Currently there is a special offer where if you buy this theme, you get all of Elegant Themes' other themes free. Eighty themes for the price of one is an exceptional deal.

Description

This is another great theme from Elegant Themes. *The Style* is a heavily image-based theme that is very simple but visually striking at the same time. The homepage consists of a very large header and a navigation bar; the rest is taken up almost completely by pictures, with short snippets of the blog post underneath them. Mousing over an image provides a larger excerpt and prompts the reader to click to read more. Each image also has the category prominently displayed on it for easy navigation.

This bold visual style is perfect for news and political blogs. In fact, any blog that is very picture oriented, such as travel blogs or personal blogs, can really benefit from this avant-garde theme style.

While there is no sidebar on the main page, there is a customizable footer where you can place info that would normally belong in the sidebar. Also, there is a sidebar within the actual blog posts. You can add various widgets, such as social buttons, recent posts, popular posts, and much more.

The Style

`http://www.elegantthemes.com/gallery/thestyle/`

Pros

- Very bold and striking visual design looks amazing
- Very easy to use and set up
- Cross-browser compatibility
- Perpetual updates
- Complete localization
- Comes in five unique colors
- Excellent support

Cons

- Homepage may be considered somewhat simplistic by some
- Doesn't have a huge amount of features and options compared to some other themes
- If you don't add a lot of images, it isn't going to look good

Conclusion

The Style manages to be both simple yet extremely bold in design. It is a definite eye-catcher that will "wow" your readers. The heavy visual design is great for holding the attention of the modern Internet generation as well. The only downside is that you're pretty much forced to use lots and lots of images — one per blog post at the bare minimum. Also, while this theme looks amazing, it isn't exactly loaded down with options and features like some other themes are. Then again, its strength lies in its simplicity. The eighty-for-one sale by Elegant Themes going on as of this writing is also an incredible offer.

Headlines

Price

Standard Package – $70

Developer Package – $150

Description

Headlines is a great looking blog theme from popular theme creator WooThemes. It features customizable header and navigation options, allowing you to alter the theme template to your liking. The homepage consists of blog post snippets with large, visually striking visuals on the left/center and a right-hand sidebar. This allows the theme to have an old-school design while incorporating a fresh modern look. You can also place a featured blog post if you want.

The sidebar widgets are very easy to customize and the unique ones included with the theme are great. One standout is the all-in-one widget that incorporates popular, latest, comments, and tags into a single tabbed widget. The blog post pages themselves look great and, once again, stick to a strong visual style while retaining a traditional blog feel.

HeadLines

```
http://www.woothemes.com/products/headlines/
```

Pros

- Successfully blends a classic and modern blog look
- A control panel that's very easy to use
- Integrated favicon and header upload
- Dynamic images options
- Various layout and navigation options
- Designed to work with Google Analytics

Cons

- May not be fancy enough for some people

- A little expensive for what you get
- Doesn't excel in any particular area

Conclusion

Headlines looks great while keeping things simple and stylish. Sticking to a classic blog format and not getting too fancy is this theme's greatest strength and its greatest weakness. It doesn't have a lot of bells and whistles compared to some blog themes, but it is still very solid and looks and functions great. The price may be a bit much for some people, though, considering the lack of features.

Rapido

Price

Limited Options - Free

Standard License - $29.95

Developer License - $49.95

Description

Rapido is a great looking theme by New WordPress Themes, known for their good work. This theme is similar to Headlines, but opts for a sleeker, more modern look. The most striking thing about Rapido is its large image slider on the homepage. It is a real eye-catcher and makes the homepage look really great while drawing attention to your featured blog posts. The header and top navigation are fairly standard, allowing you to have two navigation bars if you want. It also makes it easy to insert banner ads, social buttons, and more.

Below all of this is the blog posts section, featuring large images, post snippets, and a "read more" button. Impressively, each entry manages to fit in additional information, like date, category and comment links, without the entry seeming cluttered.

The sidebar can be configured to display even more blog entries, in a similar yet scaled down fashion. This is a great opportunity to show off some of your most popular posts. Best of all, this doesn't clutter up the homepage and actually enhances the look. You can add plenty of widgets to the sidebar of your choices as well, including Facebook widgets, tag clouds, and ads. There is also a comprehensive footer area where you can add any additional information and widgets that you want, or even more ads if you need them. This is a great blogging theme to use if you want to incorporate AdSense or other types of banner advertising.

Rapido

`http://newwpthemes.com/rapido-free-wordpress-theme/`

Pros

- Looks extremely sharp, stylish, and modern
- Very easy-to-use control panel
- Get a lot for what you pay

- Very good support system on the forums
- Compatible with all major browsers
- Easy gravitar upload for comments
- SEO optimized
- Very reasonably priced developer license

Cons

- Free version doesn't allow editing of your footer or access to the support forums
- Some people have had trouble getting the big image slider on the main page to work

Conclusion

New WordPress Themes is a great publisher and this is one of their best creations to date. Rapido is a very sharp looking theme that's great for blogging. The control panel makes it very easy for newbies to customize and use as well. One of its best features is how easy it is to insert ads, making this an excellent theme for AdSense and other ad-based sites. This theme has virtually no shortcomings if you buy the standard version. The only mishap is the fact that some people have had problems getting the slider to work. There are threads on the support forums that help with this, though.

Plugins for Blogs

When it comes to hosting a successful blog, two of the most important factors are encouraging user participation and gaining exposure. The good news is that there are plenty of plugins that can help you spread your content around the Web as well as get your readers involved.

Thank Me Later

Price

Free

Description

This plugin allows you to automatically send an email to anyone who comments on your blog. This is a great way to help people feel more involved and appreciated, encouraging further participation. Also, if you're running an e-commerce site, you can use this email to notify people of a sale, hot deal, or encourage them to sign up for your newsletter if you have one. There really is a lot you can do with this if you get creative.

Thank Me Later

`http://wordpress.org/extend/plugins/thank-me-later/`

Pros

- Allows customization of multiple emails to make them more personal
- Schedules when emails are sent
- Opens the door for tons of marketing possibilities
- Makes visitors feel appreciated

Cons

- Lacks any advanced features

Rating

Thank Me Later has a rating of 4.8 out of 5 stars.

Conclusion

This very simple plugin can have a big impact on your blog if you use it correctly. By making your visitors feel appreciated when they comment, you encourage them to further participate. And the more people who participate on your blog, the more word of it will spread and the more traffic you'll get. This plugin is also a great one for e-commerce, as it allows you to "get your foot in the door" in a somewhat subtle way for all kinds of marketing strategies.

Alternate Options

Subscribe to Comments

`http://wordpress.org/extend/plugins/subscribe-to-comments/`

– This free plugin allows visitors to subscribe to be notified of further updates in the comments section of your blog. This is very handy for getting repeat visitors to your site, which is great for SEO and encouraging participation.

Usernoise Pro Advanced Modal Feedback and Debug

`http://codecanyon.net/item/usernoise-pro-advanced-modal-feedback-debug/1420436`

– This plugin adds a unique feedback window to your blog, allowing you to more easily gather user feedback from your visitors. It is compatible with iPad and Android tablets and 99.5% of themes. This is a great way to get feedback for your blog and let your visitors recognize that you value their opinion. It costs $10 for the regular license and $50 for the extended license, and it has a five-star buyer rating.

WordPress Related Posts

Price

Free

Description

This plugin has been a huge favorite for a long time now and for good reason. When your visitors finish reading a blog post, it is important to direct them to other pages in your blog and not just leave them hanging. This plugin adds a list of related posts and thumbnails to the end of every post, ensuring that readers have somewhere to go next. It's also highly customizable and records click-through statistics as well.

WordPress Related Posts

```
http://wordpress.org/extend/plugins/wordpress-23-related-
posts-plugin/
```

Pros

- Performs an essential function
- Customizable
- Keeps track of CTR stats
- Very easy to use
- Mobile-ready

Cons

- May need to disable this on certain posts if you want to direct visitors to a specific location

Rating

WordPress Related Posts is rated 4 out of 5 stars and has been downloaded close to 600,000 times.

Conclusion

This is a great plugin to help keep visitors within your site for that extra bit of SEO juice. It is also customizable and can feature a thumbnail image to get a higher CTR. The stat tracking is great too, letting you know which links are the most effective. There really is nothing bad to say about this plugin.

Alternate Options

RelatedPosts

`http://wordpress.org/extend/plugins/related-posts/`

– This free plugin also shows related posts but does so using a sidebar widget. If you'd rather keep your related post links out of the main blog post area and in the sidebar, this may be a good choice for you. It is rated at 3.7 out of 5 stars.

Efficient Related Posts

`http://wordpress.org/extend/plugins/efficient-related-posts/`

– This is a free plugin that provides related posts, but with a twist. Instead of choosing which posts to display when a viewer clicks on the blog post, it does it only when the post is created or updated. The reason for this is that eventually other related-post plugins can slow down your site if you have hundreds of posts being accessed by tons of people each hour. If you have a very popular blog with tons of content, this is a good choice for you. It does require PHP5 to run, however.

Tweet Old Post

Price

Free

Description

This plugin is designed to allow you to get the maximum amount of value from your blog posts by tweeting them on a timed schedule. This can keep older posts relevant and have them keep bringing in traffic long after they've been published.

Tweet Old Post

```
http://wordpress.org/extend/plugins/tweet-old-
post/screenshots/
```

Pros

- Get more traffic by tweeting old posts
- Set-it-and-forget-it design
- Easy-to-use control panel

Cons

- Tweeting old posts too often could annoy your followers

Rating

This plugin has a rating of 3.8 out of 5 stars.

Conclusion

This is a great plugin when used wisely. However, if you overdo it and constantly tweet old posts, you'll be seen as a spammer. This should be used with discretion to get traffic to older posts that need some love.

Alternate Options

Tweet Posts

`http://wordpress.org/extend/plugins/tweet-posts/`

– The name says it all; when you make a blog post, it sends out a tweet to notify your followers. It also adds the appropriate metatags to activate Twitter Cards and looks at the post formatting to decide what the message should look like.

Tweetily

`http://wordpress.org/extend/plugins/tweetily-tweet-wordpress-posts-automatically/`

– Functions much the same as Tweet Old Post, but in a somewhat more random fashion. However, it also gives you more options to work with, such as the ability to set hashtags and set links back to your site. It is currently rated at 4.6 out of 5 stars.

Social Discussions

`http://wordpress.org/extend/plugins/social-discussions/`

– Not only does this free plugin allow you to enable social sharing to over 30 networks, it also allows you to automatically publish your blog posts to over 25 networks. Great for getting maximum exposure. It is currently rated at 3.9 out of 5 stars.

Media Grid

Price

Regular License - $16

Extended License - $80

Description

If you run a blog based on a service you provide, it pays to have a portfolio to show-case your samples. Media Grid makes it easy to create an attractive portfolio using vivid visual representations of your work. It features one-click setup and eight pre-defined styles. Additionally, it has full media support for video and audio, and has Pinterest, Twitter, and Facebook sharing as well. Best of all, it is optimized for mobile, allowing you to take your full portfolio with you anywhere you go, including job interviews.

Media Grid

```
http://codecanyon.net/item/media-grid-wordpress-responsive-
portfolio/2218545
```

Pros

- Create attractive visually represented portfolios
- Mobile optimization is a huge plus
- Very easy to use and newbie-friendly
- Inclusion of video and audio is also handy
- Can put together images of various dimensions, creating a very striking look

Cons

- Social media sharing is only optimized for Twitter, Facebook, and Pinterest

Rating

This plugin has a four-star buyer rating and more than 2000 downloads.

Conclusion

If you need a visually represented portfolio on your website, this is one of the best plugins you'll find. Image creation and arrangement is easy and looks great. The fact that it is mobile optimized lets you show anyone your portfolio no matter where you are; no more missed opportunities. The only drawback is that it is only optimized to share with Facebook, Twitter, and Pinterest at this time. It could benefit from share options with LinkedIn, Google+, and others. Overall, though, this is an excellent port-folio plugin.

Alternate Options

<u>Showcase</u>

`http://showcase.dev7studios.com/`

– This gallery plugin offers slightly less functionality than Media Grid, but it does have an easy-to-use drag-and-drop interface. The regular license is $14 and the ex-tended is $70, making it just slightly cheaper than Media Grid.

Fanciest Author Box

Price

Regular License - $10

Extended License - $50

Description

If you want a great looking author box at the end of every blog post, then Fanciest Author Box is a great choice. In addition to adding a professional-looking author box, it also features social media share tabs on the box, reminding readers to share your post to their favorite social media sites. Even better is the fact that if you don't want your author box at the end of your posts, you can use a widget instead of the shortcode to place it in the sidebar instead.

Fanciest Author Box

`http://codecanyon.net/item/fanciest-author-box/2504522`

Pros

- Very easy way to incorporate your author box into your blog
- Integrated social media tabs are a useful addition
- All major social media networks available for use
- Highly customizable
- Thumbnail image easy to integrate
- Can set your own color scheme
- Can be translated into other languages

Cons

- Nothing notable

Rating

This plugin has a five-star buyer rating.

Conclusion

Fanciest Author Box gets the job done, letting you add your author box either at the end of posts, the beginnings of posts, or in the sidebar. It's very easy to use, highly customizable, and the social media tabs are an excellent addition. There's nothing bad to say about this one.

Alternate Options

DT Author Box

`http://wordpress.org/extend/plugins/dt-author-box/`

– A free plugin similar to Fanciest Author Box, but geared to work for multiple authors on the same blog. It allows the standard text snippet and thumbnail images, and also has a link to the author's website and/or Twitter account. It comes in several different languages.

Fancier Author Box

`http://wordpress.org/extend/plugins/fancier-author-box/`

– Made by the same developer as Fanciest Author Box, this is a free, slightly scaled-down version. There are no widget options or social media tab options. Still, it is an adequate author box generator.

WordPress Post Planner

Price

Regular License - $16

Extended License - $80

Description

If you run a multi-author blog, it can be hard at times to keep everything organized, especially if you're working on a strict schedule. WordPress Post Planner makes it easy to keep all authors on the same page, thanks to its various features. You can assign planners, due dates, custom statuses and more to each author. It also allows you to assemble checklists to make sure all necessary tasks are completed. It offers email integration as well, making communication easy. Aside from all the editorial benefits, WordPress Post Planner also allows you to easily insert references, images, and files into your blog posts. It's multi-site compatible, making it a valuable asset if you're trying to run multiple blogs.

WordPress Post Planner

`http://codecanyon.net/item/wordpress-post-planner/2496996`

Pros

- Offers a variety of useful editorial and managerial tools
- Helps to keep multiple authors organized and on task
- Multi-site compatibility is a huge plus
- Content editing software is a great feature
- Makes life as an editor/manager much easier

Cons

- Isn't going to magically make you a good editor/manager if you don't already possess those skills
- There is a certain learning curve involved in using this plugin

Rating

This plugin has a five-star buyer rating

Conclusion

If you're an editor or manager struggling to keep everything together on a multi-author WordPress site, this plugin is a godsend. It will work wonders in keeping everyone organized and working as a team while helping to eliminate miscommunications and misunderstandings. The main drawback here is that this is only a tool; you're going to have to be the one with the managerial skills to use it. Also, while this plugin isn't overly complex, it will take some time to learn how to use it to its greatest effect.

Alternate Options

Co-Authors Plus

```
http://wordpress.org/extend/plugins/co-authors-plus/
```

– This free plugin allows you to assign multiple bylines to your blog posts if you have multiple authors. Not comparable to WordPress Post Planner but could come in handy in some situations.

Themes for Squeeze Pages

Squeeze pages are designed for one purpose: to capture leads. This usually takes the form of trying to get people to sign up to an email newsletter or sign up for a CPA offer. In any event, these are themes that have been designed for this very purpose.

OptimizePress

Price

$97

Description

OptimizePress is a theme built for multiple types of Internet marketing: sales pages, sales letters, landing pages, launch pages, one time offers and, of course, squeeze pages. The real benefit here lies in this theme's simplicity. It focuses on its task of getting people to fill out your signup form and that's it.

To facilitate this goal, the squeeze-page mode of this theme is extremely simple. It consists of a headline, video, and signup form, all above the fold. This is fully customizable, though, so if you want to swap the video out for something else, you can.

OptimizePress

`http://www.optimizepress.com/`

Pros

- Extremely simple and focused
- Like having several themes in one
- Many Internet marketers swear by this theme
- Split testing is very easy, due to the simple design
- Easy to set up and use overall

Cons

- Price may be a turn off to some

Conclusion

OptimizePress has a reputation of being a juggernaut in the world of Internet marketing; it's incredibly popular. Its simple design never deviates from its purpose. If you make a squeeze page, it works to get people to sign up with you. If you make a sales letter, it works to make sales for you. It never does anything to distract the visitor from doing what you want him or her to do; that's the power of this theme. The price is a bit steep, but you are essentially getting several themes in one, which does help to justify it a bit.

Profits Theme

Price

$97

Description

Profits Theme is similar to OptimizePress in that it is essentially several themes in one. It, too, can be used for sales letters, launch pages, etc., in addition to squeeze pages, but ultimately it is a bit more versatile and less simplistic. You can even turn it into a blog if you want.

When using this theme for a squeeze page, you have lots of options. You can set it up essentially any way you want. If you know what you're doing, this is great. If you aren't that familiar with squeeze pages, this may not be so great unless you find a tutorial online to help you out. The amount of freedom and options available may be intimidating for inexperienced users.

Profits Theme has a ton of options, features, and bells and whistles. The sheer amount of stuff you have to work with is comparable to Sahifa. You can create "buy now" buttons, Johnson boxes, testimonial boxes, guarantee seals, free trial buttons, and more — much, much, much more. This is literally just the tip of the iceberg.

You can use video, text, and columns in your squeeze pages. You can have pop-ups on your pages that prompt people to sign up for your newsletter. You can have one-time offer pages for visitors to land on after they sign up. You can have different sign up forms on different pages. All this can be done through a simple, easy to use, drag-and-drop interface that thankfully makes the complexity of this theme a little easier to bear. In fact, one testimonial states it's so easy, "a 12-year-old could do it."

Profits Theme

`http://profitstheme.com/`

Pros

- You get a lot of options and features for your money. **A lot**.
- Can create sites in many different Internet marketing styles
- Not restrictive at all; you have total freedom

- Plenty of graphics and other resources to use as well
- Looks very professional and sharp

Cons

- Can easily lead to information overload
- If you're not a web designer, you're probably going to need tutorials
- There is a learning curve involved here

Conclusion

Profits Theme's greatest strength is also its greatest weakness: you have a massive number of options and can do pretty much whatever you want. This is almost like a complete web-design kit rather than a theme, because you have so much to work with. Some marketers rate this theme as being slightly superior to OptimizePress, and you certainly get more than your money's worth here. The question is whether you are skilled enough to use it properly. If you get this theme and don't know anything about web design, you might be better off hiring someone who does to create a squeeze-page masterpiece with it.

Squeeze Theme

Price

$147

Description

Squeeze Theme is built primarily for squeeze pages and is meant to work with Squeeze Plugin, which we'll get to later. This theme is relatively simple and allows you to control various options from the control panel, including the header, appearance, display settings, footer settings, squeeze-form settings, and more.

The main page of the theme is similar to OptimizePress in simplicity, but has a few more things going on, namely a navigational bar and some things in the footer. This is all up to you; you can make it as complex or as simple as you like. You can also place the opt-in form any place you like as well, giving you plenty of options.

In addition to this, Squeeze Theme also can be converted into a sales page or a blog. There are support forums that can help with this and other questions if you get lost. The color picker makes it easy to create a nicely color-coordinated site, as well.

One of the best options that this theme offers may be its stat-tracking feature. Combined with the ability to design unlimited variants of your squeeze page in the main panel, this allows you to split test to your heart's desire and with minimum effort. This can really ramp up your opt-in rate if you stick with it.

Squeeze Theme

`http://www.squeezetheme.com/`

Pros

- Simple enough for newbies, but complex enough for web designers that want to do more with it
- Optimized for squeeze pages
- Stat tracking and unlimited variant creation makes split testing very easy
- Color picker helps to make sure the site is attractive
- Great looking overall theme design
- Support forums will help you if you get lost or stuck

Cons

- The price is a bit higher than what you'd expect
- Using this theme for anything other than squeeze pages will take a bit of a learning curve
- Some knowledge of how a squeeze page should be set up will be required

Conclusion

Squeeze Theme is a happy middle between the ultra-simplicity of OptimizePress and the hyper-complexity of Profits Theme. It gives you the freedom to do what you want, but is also simple enough that building a squeeze page shouldn't be that hard, even for beginners. The only real drawback here is the price, which is honestly a bit steep for what you get.

FlexSqueeze

Price

$127

Description

From the makers of the popular Flexibility theme comes FlexSqueeze, a theme dedicated to being a squeeze page hybrid. The reason I say "hybrid" is because, while you can make just a single-page squeeze page if you want, this theme makes it easy to work an opt-in box into a highly visible location on a blog, e-commerce store, or sales page. You have a lot of options, and this may be Profit Theme's equal in versatility, if not in sheer volume of features and options.

What sets this theme apart are the huge sub-header and footer areas that were also present in Flexibility. These areas are great for putting in whatever you want: ads, widgets, blog rolls, et cetera. But the sub-header is a particularly great place to put your opt-in box; use a video or something to give people a compelling reason to sign up before diving into the rest of your site's content.

There are quite a number of special features included with this theme. You get 10 widget locations, tons of templates to make things easy on you, unlimited colors to choose from, built in ad placement, the ability to export your settings to duplicate your sites quickly and easily, one-click color schemes, designs and layouts, and more. It also comes with full customer support in case you need help.

FlexSqueeze may just be the most well-rounded squeeze page theme available.

FlexSqueeze

`http://www.flexsqueeze.com/flexsqueeze/`

Pros

- Templates make squeeze page creation easy
- Plenty of freedom to create what you want
- Can be used to create more than just squeeze pages
- Can make really nice looking squeeze page hybrids
- Over 300 total theme options

- Comes with over 75 custom favicons, or you can upload your own
- Integrated breadcrumb navigation that's very nice
- AdSense-optimized
- Great customer support

Cons

- There will be a learning curve for newbies
- Will take some work to create a site that doesn't look simplistic

Conclusion

FlexSqueeze is very well rounded, offering plenty of options for veteran web designers to play with and easy-to-use templates for newbies. Creating a blog/squeeze-page hybrid or e-commerce/squeeze-page hybrid has never been easier. On top of that, FlexSqueeze looks great... but only if you take the time to make it look great. The templates are nice, but a bit simple looking; it's going to take some extra effort to bring out FlexSqueeze's true potential. When all is said and done, though, this squeeze-page theme is a solid choice for both newbies and veterans alike and should get more credit than it does.

Plugins for Squeeze Pages

When it comes to plugins for squeeze pages, there are several options to help you capture leads. Many revolve around getting the visitor's attention and making sure that they understand why they should sign up using your opt-in form.

PopUp Domination

Price

$77

Description

Everyone hates pop-ups, but they are one of the best ways to increase your subscriber count and capture leads. PopUp Domination is a pop-up device that looks great while displaying crucial information, like an eye-catching headline, bullet points that explain why the reader should sign up, and even a product image. PopUp Domination claims that it can't be blocked by ad-block software, and that over 15,000 of their customers experience a 500% increase in signups practically overnight.

PopUp Domination

`http://www.popupdomination.com/live/`

Pros

- Looks very professional
- Easy opt-in box integration
- Large "X" that allows readers to easily click it away if they want, so fewer people will get upset and leave your site
- Can't be blocked by ad blockers
- Lets you use copywriting elements like headlines, bullet points, etc.
- Configured with analytics to allow easy split testing for conversion optimization
- Specific page targeting
- Many customization options

Cons

- People who hate pop-ups are still going to hate this
- Somewhat expensive

Rating

None available

Conclusion

PopUp Domination looks great and allows you to create really effective lead-capturing ads. The inclusion of elements such as bullet points, headlines, and product images was a great move and can really help increase conversions. Overall, the pop-ups look great, too — very professional — and the rather large "X" in the corner is convenient for viewers who want to get rid of it right away. This is a very solid popup plugin that does everything right.

Alternate Options

Ninja Popups

```
http://codecanyon.net/item/ninja-popups-for-
wordpress/3476479
```

– A cheaper alternative to PopUp Domination with even greater functionality, this $16 plugin can pretty much do it all. Key features include the ability to put social "like" buttons in your pop-up and the fact that the plugin is already optimized for integration with several of the most popular autoresponder services, like Aweber and MailChimp. It even allows you to lock pages of your website until readers either click a "like" button or sign up using your opt-in form.

WordPress PopUp

```
http://wordpress.org/extend/plugins/wordpress-popup/
```

– This free pop-up plugin doesn't have autoresponder integration, but it can still come in handy. It can be set on a timer to pop up after visitors have been on a page for a certain amount of time. It has an option that allows visitors to click it away so that it never displays again, and another option to select which visitors see it. It's currently rated at 4.1 out of 5 stars.

Optin Revolution

```
http://wordpress.org/extend/plugins/optin-revolution/
```

– One of the few free popup plugins that's comparable to PopUp Domination and Ninja Popups. This one has a lot of functionality and options, as well as the all-important ability to integrate your opt-in box directly into the pop-up. There are video training tutorials on the site as well, making it very newbie-friendly. This plugin has a rating of 4.9 out of 5 stars.

<u>WPSubscribers</u>

`http://www.wpsubscribers.com/`

– This plugin offers plenty of options and features, but the one that stands out the most is the fact that you can place your pop-ups on any page or post you want, allowing you to get more targeted and increase your signup rate. It has tracking analytics, can auto-fill your visitor's name and email into the opt-in form, and allows visitors to subscribe while commenting. This plugin costs $47 for the triple license and $97 for an unlimited license that allows you to use it on an unlimited number of sites and gives you top customer support priority.

MyMail

Price

Regular License - $25

Extended License not available

Description

MyMail is a newsletter management system. It gives you a wide variety of handy options so that you can have better control over email list campaigns from your WordPress dashboard. Its tracking options will help you to optimize your campaign, and you can use the scheduling feature to set up emails to go out when you want them to. You can also send out specific emails to specific people on your list. Another great feature is that you can actually create your newsletter right in your WordPress dashboard. There is also an option that checks your emails to make sure nothing will get it sent to the recipient's spam folder.

MyMail

```
http://codecanyon.net/item/mymail-email-newsletter-plugin-
for-wordpress/3078294
```

Pros

- Lots of customization options
- Feature that checks for things that will put your email in spam folders is invaluable
- Being able to manage your campaign from your WordPress dashboard is very convenient
- Has double opt-in support
- Has multi-language support

Cons

- May take a bit of a learning curve to figure out how to use all of the options

Rating

This plugin has a 5 out of 5 buyer rating.

Conclusion

Managing email newsletters from your autoresponder account can be annoying, especially since some of them can be hard to learn. This plugin not only simplifies a lot of that, it also adds a lot of functionality that most autoresponder services lack. The ability to pre-check your emails for spam factors is great, and the tracking options are also a must-have. This is a very good all-around newsletter management plugin.

Alternate Options

WordPress Email Newsletter Plugin

```
http://codecanyon.net/item/wordpress-email-newsletter-
plugin/149180
```

– This is another plugin that has a ton of options and functionality for creating and managing a newsletter from your WordPress dashboard. It has scheduling, templates, and bounce tracking, just to name a few features. It costs $25 for the standard license and $125 for the extended. It also has a buyer rating of 4 out of 5 stars.

Email Newsletter

```
http://wordpress.org/extend/plugins/email-newsletter/
```

– This plugin allows you to send emails to registered members of your site, essentially allowing you to have a newsletter without the need for an autoresponder. It is kind of basic in comparison to some of the others, but it is free.

Newsletter

```
http://wordpress.org/extend/plugins/newsletter/
```

– Another basic WordPress-based email newsletter system. This one allows unlimited emails and unlimited subscribers and offers configurable themes to work with. It is rated at 4 out of 5 stars and has been downloaded over 200,000 times.

Squeeze Plugin

Price

$97 for unlimited use

Description

This plugin is meant for use with the FlexSqueeze theme, but in truth it can turn any WordPress theme into a squeeze page. The drag-and-drop interface lets you build a squeeze page in minutes, inserting video and autoresponder codes with a click of your mouse. The overall appearance of the squeeze page looks very simple, but it gets the job done.

Squeeze Plugin

`http://www.squeezetheme.com/`

Pros

- Very easy to use and newbie-friendly
- Simple design is free of distractions for visitors
- Video integration is very easy to use
- Can be used to turn any page on your site into a squeeze page

Cons

- Somewhat expensive
- Some people may not like the simple design

Rating

None available

Conclusion

Squeeze Plugin is a great squeeze-page creation plugin. It covers all the basics and is extremely newbie-friendly. The main drawback is that you're paying close to $100 and don't exactly get a huge amount of bells and whistles in return. Still, the plugin does what it is designed to do, and does it very well.

Alternate Options

<u>WordPress Squeeze Page Plugin</u>

`http://www.wpsqueezepage.com/`

– This plugin allows you to build just about any kind of squeeze page you could imagine. It has tons of options, including the ability to integrate Google Content Experiments for easy split testing and optimization. It also comes with special members-only support area access. This plugin costs $47.

<u>WordPress Landing Pages</u>

`http://wordpress.org/extend/plugins/landing-pages/`

– This free plugin allows you to create a variety of landing pages for your WordPress site. It offers stat tracking for easy split testing, templates, and the ability to easily clone landing pages. It has a rating of 4.7 out of 5 stars, but only three ratings.

<u>Simple Newsletter Signup</u>

`http://wordpress.org/extend/plugins/simple-newsletter-signup/`

– This free plugin lets you insert opt-in forms quickly and easily. It's optimized to work with third-party autoresponders, such as MailChimp, Constant Contact, and others. It is a relatively new plugin with no ratings yet, though it has close to 1,000 downloads.

Themes for AdSense

AdSense is a classic way to make money using WordPress. AdSense ads can be inserted into just about any type of site, and you make money when people click on them. However, some themes have been created specifically with AdSense revenue in mind.

HeatMap

Price

$67 for lifetime membership

Description

Developers and analysts often use what are known as "heat maps" to map out the spots on a web page where an ad will get the most clicks and make the most money. The HeatMap theme is built around that principle, setting things up and guiding you so that you place your ads in the statistically most successful positions. It also has a variety of other useful features, such as ad rotation, authority skins to make your site look great, social media button integration, site cloning, and internal SEO features, just to name a few.

How the overall look and design of the site turns out is up to you. You have a huge amount of freedom to make your site how you want. HeatMap also caters to affiliate sites, squeeze pages, sales letters, and more if you want to create those types of websites as well.

HeatMap

`http://heatmaptheme.com/`

Pros

- Very targeted ad positioning that's great for newbies
- Loaded with features and options
- Can create and optimize many different sites for ads
- SEO and social integration is a huge plus
- Logo and favicon uploaders
- Page templates are a time-saver

Cons

- The number of options and amount of freedom can be intimidating for newbies

Conclusion

HeatMap has been a favorite among AdSense marketers for some time now, and for good reason. It takes you by the hand and shows you exactly where you should be placing your ads, leading to higher click-through rates. The only issue is that the huge number of options and the ability to customize your site any way you want may leave some people feeling lost.

Adsense Pro Ultimate

Price

Regular License - $69

Developer License - $149

Description

This theme focuses on being as simple as possible, allowing users to create sites that don't distract from the ads for a higher CTR. This also has the side effect of producing very fast-loading sites, since they aren't bogged down by extra bells and whistles. Other features include AdSense integration, favicon integration, analytics/stat management, and tracking code integration.

Adsense Pro Ultimate

`http://ctr-themes.com/themes/adsense-pro-ultimate/`

Pros

- Simple design for fast loading and maximum CTR
- Analytics and stat tracking helps you optimize your ads and ad placement
- Very versatile overall

Cons

- Simplistic look may be considered dated by some
- Optimal ad placement will take some know-how to implement

Conclusion

Adsense Pro Ultimate is a great theme for a pure AdSense site. It covers all the basics very well and has some great features like stat tracking and code integration. The main issue here is that it really isn't suitable for anything other than a pure AdSense site that uses a blog format. Then again, if your goal is to make money with AdSense, you probably don't need anything more fancy, anyway.

MaxSense

Price

$69 for lifetime membership

Description

MaxSense is an AdSense theme designed to focus around a blogging platform. Since you will need compelling content to draw people to your site, this is a reasonable approach. The placement of ads can be edited to your liking, allowing you to place ads in sidebars. It also comes with integrated analytics and stat management as well.

The sleek and modern look of the theme gives it a slight edge over themes like Adsense Pro Ultimate in the overall appearance department. The use of thumbnails really enhances the main page and keeps visitors from bouncing.

MaxSense

`http://www.adsensepress.com/maxsense-wordpress-theme`

Pros

- Looks sharp and modern
- Great for blogs that want to incorporate AdSense
- Analytics and stat tracking are plusses
- Compatible with all major browsers
- Footer area is fully customizable

Cons

- Ad placement seems somewhat limited
- Seems more like a blog theme than an AdSense theme

Conclusion

While this theme does look great, I can't help but feel that it leans more toward being a blog theme with AdSense thrown in as an afterthought. This is mainly due to the limited way in which ad placement is implemented. It has some nice features, though, and is easy to set up. If you run a blog and want to put ads on it, this isn't a bad choice.

CTR Theme

Price

$67. However, you can get it for free when subscribing to one of CTR Theme's hosted plans, which start at $4.99 a month.

Description

Despite its simplicity, CTR Theme manages to look very professional and attractive, albeit in a basic kind of way. Its ad placement strategy is based on the placement recommendations from Google AdSense, so it comes from a reliable source. It also has an ad placement randomizer that helps to prevent readers from automatically filtering out the ads in their mind. Other features include super-fast load times, social media integration, and multiple sub-themes.

CTR Theme comes with several layout options. Some feature images, others have a prominent header, and there's still another that's just text. In each case, the ads are placed in very prominent locations as dictated by Google. At the same time, the ads don't come across as being obnoxious, which is great. To the untrained eye, some of these layout options don't even look like pure AdSense sites.

CTR Theme

`http://www.ctrtheme.com/`

Pros

- Simple yet attractive
- Multiple layout options
- AdSense integration based on Google's recommendations
- Powerful core features
- Easy to use
- Comes with a bonus: AdSense Link-Building Secrets guide

Cons

- This is a pure AdSense theme, so it may not be good for affiliate sites, dedicated blogs, etc.

Conclusion

CTR Theme is a very focused, attractive AdSense theme. It aims for one thing, getting people to click on ads, and it does it well. It has plenty of features and options, including several layouts, so you can set the site up the way you want within certain parameters. Because of its simplicity, it is very newbie-friendly and easy to use. However, due to its ultra-focused nature, it probably isn't what you want if you're trying to put ads on a popular blog or your affiliate site. If you're trying to concentrate on AdSense revenue, though, this is one of the best choices available. Also, an unlimited site license is included with your purchase so you can create an army of AdSense sites using this theme if you want.

Plugins for AdSense

There are a variety of plugins that make using AdSense a bit easier. Some of these are redundant with certain AdSense theme functions, while others work to complement AdSense themes.

Click Missile

Price

$47, but reduced to $27 as part of a special offer

Description

Click Missile was created by the developers of HeatMap. It shows you exactly where the hottest spots on your site are for ad placement, similar to the way that HeatMap functions. The benefit here is that this plugin can be used for any site, making it great for hybrid sites. For example, if you wanted to put AdSense on your affiliate site, this would show you where to place your ads for maximum CTR.

Click Missile

```
http://heatmaptheme.com/click-missile-ads-placement-plugin-
for-wordpress/
```

Pros

- Shows you where to place your ads. Great for AdSense newbies
- Works with any site
- Optimized for mobile devices
- Allows you to place ads for certain categories and tags

Cons

- AdSense veterans who already know where to put their ads may not find this as useful

Rating

None available

Conclusion

Click Missile is great for anyone just getting started with AdSense and ad revenue generation as a whole. It shows you exactly where you should be placing your ads for the highest click-through rate and allows you to place ads by category or for posts with certain tags. Being mobile optimized is also a huge plus. The only problem is that veterans of AdSense and other programs might not find it all that useful if they already know where to put ads.

Google AdSense Plugin

`http://wordpress.org/extend/plugins/adsense-plugin/`

–This is a free plugin with basic functionality. It allows you to place ads on your site quickly and easily, and has some customization options as well. Also features multi-language capabilities.

All in One AdSense and YPN Pro

`http://wordpress.org/extend/plugins/all-in-one-adsense-and-ypn-pro/`

– This is a free plugin that allows you to place not only AdSense ads on your site, but ads from the Yahoo! Partner Network as well. Comes with options that grant you a lot of control over where your ads are placed on your site and an ad randomizer to prevent readers from developing "ad blindness."

Easy AdSense

`http://wordpress.org/extend/plugins/easy-adsense-lite/`

– Here is another free plugin. This one has the benefit of enforcing Google's "only three ad blocks per page" rule to keep you out of trouble. It also displays ad blocks based on post length, keeping your layout looking nice and clutter-free. It has a rating of 3.2 out of 5 stars.

WP Auto Post ADS

`http://wordpress.org/extend/plugins/wp-ads-auto-post/`

– A very basic free plugin that allows you to add AdSense to your site automatically. Features iFrame, HTML, and JavaScript support. This plugin is rated 5 out of 5 stars by three voters total.

Google Adsense Report Pro

Price

Free

Description

If you don't have a fancy ad plugin or theme that tracks your stats automatically, this plugin can be a great help. Google Adsense Report Pro allows you to track various ad data in your dashboard and even provides graphics and dollar currency support. It is also available in Spanish.

Google Adsense Report Pro

`http://wordpress.org/extend/plugins/google-adsense-report-pro/`

Pros

- Helps you optimize your CTR by tracking your stats
- Very simple and easy to use
- Makes a great addition to any theme or AdSense insertion plugin that doesn't feature tracking

Cons

- It's nothing but a tracking plugin

Rating

Has a five-star rating, but only one person has rated it so far. Has over 2,000 downloads.

Conclusion

A very handy free plugin if you need stat tracking and analytics. The data is easy to read and understand. The only drawback is that it doesn't do anything else. Then again, it wasn't designed to.

Alternate Options

Ad Logger

`http://wordpress.org/extend/plugins/ad-logger/`

– This free plugin collects data not just on AdSense clicks, but on Amazon, Facebook, and Twitter as well. It also has a bombing prevention function that stops bots or malicious people from clicking your ads repeatedly, which can get you in trouble with Google. The general concept is solid, but the implementation of this plugin may be a bit too advanced for some, since it saves the data to your MySQL database. It has a rating of 2.6 out of 5 stars.

Google AdSense and Google Analytics Remover

```
http://wordpress.org/extend/plugins/google-adsense-and-
google-analytics-remover/
```

– Your AdSense data can become skewed when you log in to your WordPress account to work on it. This free plugin blocks out ads and removes data collection when you're logged into your WordPress account to keep your data as accurate as possible.

Better AdSense Targeting

Price

Free

Description

One of the main keys to success with AdSense is being able to target your ads to your website's demographic and content. This plugin works to improve your targeting and ensure that your ads match your content by allowing you to select which areas of your site are used to select ads from the network.

Better AdSense Targeting

```
http://wordpress.org/extend/plugins/better-adsense-
targeting/
```

Pros

- Increases ad targeting, which increases CTR
- Great for sites that have content that is unrelated to the main theme
- Easy to use

Cons

- No real special features or options

Rating

Better AdSense Targeting is rated 4.7 out of 5 stars.

Conclusion

This is a very handy plugin for sites that have a lot of varied content, such as personal blogs or travel blogs. Better AdSense Targeting makes sure that the ads displayed are ones that are relevant to the reader's interests, helping to increase CTR. It doesn't do anything fancy, but then again, it really doesn't need to.

Komoona's Google AdSense Companion

Price

Free

Description

This is another plugin that allows you to place AdSense ads on your WordPress site, but this one works a little differently. In addition to basic AdSense functionality, it also allows you to set a minimum price for ads. If the AdSense ads that are to be displayed have a lower payout than the set price, Komoona will replace them with alternate, higher value ads. In addition to this, it can also be configured to allow independent advertisers to create and upload ads automatically. This plugin is available in over 20 languages.

Komoona's Google AdSense Companion

```
http://wordpress.org/extend/plugins/komoona-ads-google-
adsense-companion/
```

Pros

- Has basic AdSense insertion functionality
- Allows you to regulate the value of your ads to some degree
- Simplifies working with independent advertisers on your site
- Relatively easy to use and has detailed instructions on how to set it up

Cons

- Some may view this as unnecessary

Rating

This plugin has a rating of 3.7 out of 5 stars

Conclusion

Komoona is an interesting plugin that provides a unique function. It could increase your overall revenue stream, but some may feel that it is unnecessary. It is free, though, so it wouldn't hurt to give it a try if you're interested.

Plugins for Forums, Chat Rooms, and Membership Sites

I won't be going over any themes for these types of sites because really just about any theme could be used. It is the plugins that you use that will give the functionality you need for these types of options on your WordPress site.

Simple:Press

Price

Free for the core plugin.

Support plugins require a membership: $39 for a two-month plan or $99 for a twelve-month plan

Description

The Simple:Press plugin adds a forum to any WordPress site with its own forum template/theme. It has sub-forum support and a variety of handy features, such as forum ranks/badges for members, automatic thumbnail and pop-up enlargement, user-defined signatures, smileys and custom smiley upload, and much more. In short, it has pretty much everything you could ever want in a forum, including security, SEO, and language features.

The overall look of the forum is simple and clean, but it's also highly customizable. You can choose the colors, set thumbnail graphics for each sub-forum, and create your forum in any way you choose. It's nothing fancy, visually speaking, but it doesn't really need to be.

This plugin is designed to work with a ton of support plugins for additional functionality. Examples include private messaging, post previews, polls, an admin bar, CAPTCHA, font resizing, and post rating. (And that's just the tip of the iceberg.) Furthermore, these plugins are all made by the same developer, so you won't' have to worry about compatibility issues. However, it must be mentioned that access to the support plugins requires a membership fee. ($39 for 2 months; $99 for 12 months)

Simple Press

`http://simple-press.com/`

Pros

- Very well rounded forum plugin
- Tons of options and features
- You can select which features you want using the additional plugin system
- Forum looks clean and simple
- Core plugin is free

Cons

- Forum setup may be considered basic looking by some
- Must pay a membership fee for support plugins

Rating

None available

Conclusion

This is an excellent forum plugin that has all the functionality you could ever want in a forum. The design looks very clean and is easy to use, not cluttered and clunky like some forum designs. The only thing holding this product back is the fact that you have to pay a membership fee for support plugins that have important functions. While you do get access to all the support plugins for a very reasonable price, the re-occurring fee will turn some people off.

Alternate Options

Forums

`http://wordpress.org/extend/plugins/zingiri-forum/`

– This free plugin is an easy way to add the very popular myBB forum software to WordPress. While the forums look very modern and eye-catching, and the plugin does have good functionality, some have reported encountering bugs. Still, this is good forum software for free, especially if you're a fan of myBB. It has a rating of 2.7 out of 5 stars.

Mingle Forum

`http://wordpress.org/extend/plugins/mingle-forum/`

– This is a unique forum plugin for WordPress that has more features than you'd expect from a free product. You can choose from several skins, all of which look really good. Other notable features are the use of BB code, hot/very-hot topic icons, user signatures, SEO friendly URLs, and quick reply, just to name a few. This plugin has a rating of 3.9 out of 5 stars and there is plenty of support for it on its main site, including support forums.

<u>Vanilla Forums</u>

`http://vanillaforums.org/`

– This is a professional-level forum plugin that is actually more than just a plugin. To get this to work, you're going to have to go through some technical stuff, especially if you're planning on installing this on your own host. If you are technically skilled enough to do this, you'll be rewarded with a *very* high-end forum with excellent functionality and options. This plugin has both free and paid versions.

Premise

Price

$165

Description

Premise is a plugin designed for membership sites that offers plenty of features to help facilitate long-term profitability. It allows you to create a variety of landing pages, using video content and more. It also has templates for each page type, along with more than 1,100 custom graphics. It comes with an e-book, "The Premise Copywriting Approach," and even has copywriting tips inside WordPress to help you better convince people to sign up with you.

On top of all that, it allows you to accept recurring payments and drip-feed content on a precise schedule. It's got built-in checkout pages and the ability to set up password-protected content libraries, too. You'll also be happy to know that it works with any WordPress theme or framework. Furthermore, it also allows easy split testing and optimization.

Premise

`http://getpremise.com/`

Pros

- Many helpful features
- Geared towards making you as successful as possible
- Easy to use
- Works with any theme or framework
- Integrated checkout page and payment-processing with PayPal and Authorize.net
- Can create private forum areas

Cons

- Takes some web design skill to fully implement all of its features

Rating

None available

Conclusion

Premise is a very robust membership site plugin that does practically everything you could possibly want it to do. The integrated checkout and payment processing is amazing and the copywriting tips and e-book will work wonders for you if you don't know anything about writing copy. The developers of this plugin have gone out of their way to try and make you successful. The only drawback is that it will take some web design knowledge to implement all of the features on your site; this isn't the kind of plugin that you just install and you're good to go.

Alternate Options

Membership Lite/Membership Pro

`http://wordpress.org/extend/plugins/membership/`

– This plugin adds a lot of membership functionality to your WordPress site by providing subscribers access to content based on their membership level. The Pro version ($19 or $39.50, depending on what you get) allows unlimited membership levels and subscription levels, while the free Lite version is limited to two. A very solid membership plugin. The Lite version is rated 3.9 out of 5 stars.

Magic Members

`http://www.magicmembers.com/`

– This is a very comprehensive membership plugin with plenty of features, such as sales reports, multi-lingual integration, Simple:Press forum integration, controlled content management, payment integrating, S3 Amazon support, and much, much more. It also has excellent support, including tutorials, training, updates, and customer service. A single license costs $97; you can get a three-user license for $197 and unlimited for $297. This is an extremely powerful membership plugin.

SabaiDiscuss

Price

$20

Description

This plugin adds a question-and-answer area, sort of like Yahoo! Answers, to your WordPress site. The layout is very clean and organized, as the minimalist style works well with just about any theme. Other features include a voting system, easy moderation, an abuse reporting function, profile pages, a reputation system for members, and an easy cloning system.

SabaiDiscuss

`http://sabaidiscuss.com/`

Pros

- Simple and easy to use for administrators and users
- Question-and-answer style is very popular
- Many options and features
- Looks great with any theme

Cons

- More simplistic than a true forum

Rating

None available

Conclusion

SabaiDiscuss is a great plugin if you want to add a Q&A section to your site in the vein of Yahoo! Answers. It allows users to interact with one another in a simple yet fun way while sharing useful information. This is, of course, much less functional than a true forum but its charm is in its simplicity.

Alternate Options

Question and Answer Forum

```
http://wordpress.org/extend/plugins/question-and-answer-
forum/
```

– A free plugin that also functions with a sort of question-and-answer format. This one is very basic, but does allow user profile pages and customization by theme. It also comes with a neat widget that will show the last five questions. It has a rating of 3.8 out of 5 stars.

SD Questions and Answers

```
http://wordpress.org/extend/plugins/sd-questions-and-
answers/
```

– This free plugin has basic Q&A functionality, but the catch is that only the admin can create questions for the guests to answer. In that regard, it functions more like a feedback or polling option than a true discussion forum. Still, it can be a great way to encourage interaction on your site without letting the guests get out of control.

WP Feedback and Survey Manager

```
http://wordpress.org/extend/plugins/wp-feedback-survey-
manager/
```

– This is a free plugin that allows you to collect feedback and survey data from your site. It is similar to SD Questions and Answers, but in this case it's more for data collection than encouraging interaction. The data gathered is displayed in a variety of charts and graphs. This plugin has a rating of 4.8 out of 5 stars.

Chat and Chat Pro

Price

Free/$19

Description

Chat and Chat Pro are plugins designed to create direct live chat on your WordPress site. With the chat box enabled, you can easily communicate directly with your members and they can communicate with each other. This has great application for both social and commercial interests. The free variant offers just a basic chat box, while the Pro version offers many advanced features, such as the ability for any Facebook/Twitter user to join the conversation, selecting which roles are mods, changing colors, enabling emoticons, disabling avatars, and archiving chats.

Chat and Chat Pro

`http://premium.wpmudev.org/project/wordpress-chat-plugin/`

Pros

- Free version gets the job done and the Pro version has a lot of handy features
- Good for both commercial and social sites
- Very easy to use

Cons

- Free version is obviously designed to make you want to purchase the Pro version

Rating

Free version is rated at 4.4 out of 5 stars

Conclusion

Chat and Chat Pro are both great chat plugins. While the free variant is a bit basic, the Pro version has plenty of great options and functionality. While the free version is intended to get you to buy the Pro version, it isn't a bad deal at all at $19 if you want a chat program on your site with more advanced functions.

Alternate Options

Quick Chat

`http://wordpress.org/extend/plugins/quick-chat/`

– This is a very comprehensive free plugin that features a decent number of features like multi-lingual capabilities, the ability to block certain words, and the ability of an admin to ban users from chat. It is rated 4.5 out of 5 stars and has been downloaded over 100,000 times.

Banckle Live Chat

`http://wordpress.org/extend/plugins/banckle-live-chat-for-wordpress/`

– This is a free live chat plugin that gives you plenty of administrative control. You can define filter rules, create notifications, and even create surveys for post-chat sessions. It is also fully customizable.

HTML5 Online Chat Widget, aka RumbleTalk

`http://wordpress.org/extend/plugins/rumbletalk-chat-a-chat-with-themes/`

– This free plugin features Facebook and Twitter integration and has a strong focus on being mobile-friendly. It also has a theme library, an option to ban trolls, a private chat feature, and supports 29 languages. It's rated at 4.1 out of 5 stars.

Final Word

As you can see, there are plenty of plugins and themes for WordPress, and this is just a small fraction of what is available. There are literally thousands and thousands to choose from, making it easy to find something for your unique needs.

I did my best to present some of the most popular plugins as well as some alternate options that you may not have heard of before. If you're looking for something specific and didn't see it listed here, try searching through the various sites listed in the resources section.

Ultimately, this goes to show just how versatile and easy WordPress is to use as a website-building platform. There really are options for everyone and every type of site imaginable. Finding the perfect plugins and themes to build your site the way you want has never been easier.

If you want more information on how to build WordPress websites and keep them safe from hackers, check out my other books, *WordPress Domination* and *WordPress Security*. They complement this book perfectly and will help you use WordPress to its fullest potential.

Thanks for reading. I'm always glad to have the opportunity to share information regarding this incredibly customizable and easy-to-use website-building platform. Whether you're building a site for fun or for profit, I wish you the best of luck!

Your Friend,

Lambert Klein

www.LambertKlein.com

Resources

Didn't find what you were looking for in the guide? Try these sources; you'll find access to thousands of great plugins and themes for your WordPress site. Enjoy!

Themes

- ThemeGrade.com
  ThemeForest.net
- NewWPThemes.com
- ElegantThemes.com
- WooThemes.com
- SMThemes.com
- ThemeFuse.com
- TemplateMonster.com
- ThemifyMe.com/themes

Plugins

- CodeCanyon.net
- WordPress.org/extend/plugins
- Yoast.com/WordPress
- StudioPress.com/plugins
- ElegantThemes.com/plugins

If you have found this book useful then please leave an unbiased review on Amazon at:

`http://www.amazon.com/dp/B00B35YH4G`

WordPress Top Plugins and Themes Review Book

Thanks!

CPSIA information can be obtained at www.ICGtesting.com
Printed in the USA
BVOW050959250213

314120BV00003B/89/P